MW00487569

LETTERS FOR LAWYERS

Essential Communications for Clients, Prospects, and Others

2nd Edition

THOMAS E. KANE

ABA General Practice, Solo & Small Firm Section

Cover design by ABA Publishing.

The materials contained herein represent the opinions of the authors and editors and should not be construed to be the action of either the American Bar Association or the General Practice, Solo and Small Firm Section unless adopted pursuant to the bylaws of the Association.

Nothing contained in this book is to be considered as the rendering of legal or financial advice for specific cases, and readers are responsible for obtaining such advice from their own legal or financial counsel. This book and any forms and agreements herein are intended for educational and informational purposes only

© 2004 American Bar Association. All rights reserved.
Printed in the United States of America.

08 07 06   5 4 3

Library of Congress Cataloging-in-Publication Data

Kane, Thomas E.
Letters for laywers : essential communications for clients, prospects, and others / by Thomas E. Kane.— 2nd ed.
    p. cm.
   ISBN 1-59031-267-8 (pbk.)
    1. Communication in law—United States. 2. Attorney and client—United States. 3. Legal correspondence—United States. 4. Form letters—United States. I. Title.

KF320.L48K36 2004
808'.06634—dc22   2003018532

Discounts are available for books ordered in bulk. Special consideration is given to state bars, CLE programs, and other bar-related organizations. Inquire at ABA Publishing, Book Publishing, American Bar Association, 750 North Lake Shore Drive, Chicago, Illinois 60611.

www.ababooks.org

Contents

CHAPTER 2

Communication with Employees and Prospective Employees 79

CHAPTER 3

Communication with Prospective Clients and Other Contacts 101

CHAPTER 4

Introduction to the Second Edition

The legal industry continues to change dramatically, with mergers and consolidations in some markets, and firms going out of business in others. Client demands on professional service providers continue to put pressure on lawyers to be more responsive to their clients' needs. Clients simply expect their lawyers to be responsive, efficient, and cost-conscious. They also expect to hear from them. Communication with clients has never been more important.

In this second edition of *Letters for Lawyers: Essential Communications for Clients, Prospects, and Others*, you will find changes in at least 80 percent of the letters. There have been many changes in our world since the first edition, not the least of which is the prolific use of the Internet and, especially, e-mail. While the letters in this book can be used in the form of e-mail, I still believe in the importance of sending letters in the old-fashioned way. E-mail has proliferated to the point where many people are either annoyed by the intrusion or are overwhelmed by the sheer number of e-mails they receive each day.

As you go through *Letters for Lawyers,* consider your clients' preference for the mode of communication first and foremost. The benefits of increasing your communications with clients may be lost otherwise.

Changes to the second edition also include new letters, which were added in several areas. For example, one of the most effective ways to enhance relationships with current clients is by instituting an in-person interview program. It also is a surefire way to obtain additional work from clients. Several letters were added in Chapter One to facilitate such a program. Letters were also added in the area of client feedback following completion of a matter, including an End of Matter Confirmation Letter. Other letters were added in the areas of legal services proposals and presentations, responses to requests for charitable sponsorships, and a letter requesting a rating review by Martindale-Hubbell.

The need for lawyers to effectively communicate with clients is as important as ever today. And the reasoning for increasing communications with clients, spelled out in the Introduction to the First Edition that follows, is just as valid today as the day it was written. May *Letters for Lawyers, 2nd edition* help you in these critical aspects of your profession.

For your convenience, this second edition comes with a CD-ROM containing all letters and forms in both MS Word and WordPefect formats. This should help you get started right away in improving your communications with those who can helpyou develop and enhance your client relationships.

Thomas E. Kane
tkane@kaneconsultinginc.com
941.376.3366

An Introduction to Written Communications

Why Frequent Communication with Clients and Others Is important

Frequent, effective written communication is vital to the successful practice of law. *Letters for Lawyers: Essential Communications for Clients, Prospects, and Others* was written to ease the task of communicating with clients and prospective clients, referral sources, employees, the media, and others. By using the handbook as a resource tool and undertaking its program of frequent and effective communication, you can build strong client relationships, generate referrals and attract new clients, improve personnel management, smoothly handle routine matters, and establish or strengthen your public relations efforts.

Frequent Communication Is Part of Client Service

Why is frequent communication so important? The answer is simple: Communication is a crucial aspect of client service. The best lawyers understand that "legal services" is not one word. That is, legal service is not just the rendering of a legal "product." No sensible marketing professional would contend that excellent legal work is any less important today than it always has been. In fact, it may be more important now in light of increased competition. That is the "legal" part. Equally important, if not more so to many clients, is how the "service" is rendered. Did the lawyer *communicate,* keep the client informed, send documents, provide background information,

explain changes in the law, and so forth? Most clients who are unhappy with their lawyer mention poor service or communication as the primary reason.

Many state bar associations have pointed out that 70 to 80 percent of the grievances filed against lawyers are due to a "lack of communication," "inattention to the client's matter," "failure to communicate," or "failure to keep clients advised about their matter." Often the lawyer *is* paying attention to a client's matter quite appropriately, but *is not communicating* often enough with the client to instill confidence that he or she is doing so.

Further, the grievance, although not malpractice on its face, can lead to the filing of a malpractice action by a frustrated client. Even if the lawsuit does not succeed, it must be defended—at a cost—and undoubtedly will lead to greater scrutiny by the lawyer's professional liability insurance carrier. In short, a lawyer's lack of communication can lead to higher insurance rates and lost referrals in addition to the time and money she or he may need to spend defending themselves in court. This book was designed to help lawyers solve their communication problems quickly and easily.

Frequent Communication Helps to Solve the Intangibility Problem

One difference between a "product" and a "service" is the lack of tangible evidence that a service has been provided. This difference creates unique marketing challenges for many professionals, including lawyers. One of the easiest ways for lawyers to increase the tangible evidence of a service is to increase the frequency of written communications.

The three most important factors for a successful real estate venture are location, location, location—the three most important factors when it comes to legal services marketing are **contact, contact, contact**. Written communication offers one way to keep in contact with those who use, or could use, your services. Written communication does not replace personal contact, but is an excellent complement to face-to-face meetings. Effective written communication should be undertaken at every opportunity to show a client that the relationship is important and his or her business is appreciated.

Your goal should be to communicate, in writing, with key clients and referral sources at least six times per year, and with other clients and referral sources on a regular but less frequent basis. The important point is not the precise time frame so much as remembering to communicate often.

Using *Letters for Lawyers*

This handbook contains various communication tools, including business letters, announcement cards, invitations, survey forms, response cards, press releases, and thank you notes. These tools are organized into four chapters.

Chapter One focuses on communication with clients and referral sources. Communication with employees and prospective employees is the subject of Chapter Two. Chapter Three deals with prospective clients and other contacts, and Chapter Four addresses communication with the media.

Conveniently included with the handbook are WordPerfect® versions of all letters on diskette, to make them even easier to use and tailor to your own practice. Don't let the merge codes and macro functions deter you! Refer to *WordPerfect® Shortcuts for Lawyers—Learning Merge and Macros in One Hour,* by Carol Woodbury (Chicago: American Bar Association, 1994).

All letters should be reviewed with your state's Code of Professional Responsibility in mind, since there are different requirements that apply, especially when communicating with non-clients.

Study the handbook, considering how each of the formats could apply to your unique situation. Develop your own lists of clients, referral sources, prospective clients, and media contacts. Then communicate with them and enjoy the benefits of effective communication!

Communication with Clients and Referral Sources

ood communicators are successful business generators, as well as being better service providers. Lawyers who are effective communicators look for opportunities to contact clients because they know that the majority of new business comes from existing clients—whether that be in the nature of new client work or client-referred work.

This chapter includes many revised letters and forms designed to handle the routine business matters that lawyers encounter repeatedly. There are letters dealing with the financial aspects of law practice, including billing, collection, and retainer fees. Further, there are letters to offer apologies, congratulations, or thanks; to confirm or change seminar reservations or meeting times; to announce mergers or buyouts; and to request referrals. There are letters on a more personal note, involving holiday greetings and offering condolences. Also, there are several formats for open-house invitations, along with a client satisfaction survey, a tax-time reminder, and a cover letter to use when sending items of interest. Finally, this edition adds letters dealing with end-of-matter questionnaires and in-person client interviews—one of the most effective business development tools.

These letters will help you improve your client communications. The result will be stronger, more efficient client relationships.

CHAPTER

1

LETTERS FOR
LAWYERS
Essential
Communications
for Clients,
Prospects, and
Others

Client Satisfaction Survey–
Cover Letter

FIELD {Date}

FIELD {Name}
FIELD {Company Name}
FIELD {Address}
FIELD {City, State, Zip Code}

Dear FIELD {Salutation}:

(Firm Name) is committed to providing high-quality service to all of our clients. In order to help us achieve and sustain that goal, we would like your feedback regarding our services.

Please take a few minutes to complete the enclosed [questionnaire OR client satisfaction survey]. Your answers will help us identify areas where we are doing a good job, as well as areas needing improvement. [We ask that you return your responses by (date) in the enclosed self-addressed envelope OR We have contracted with XYZ Consulting Company, an independent firm, to assist us with the survey. We ask that you return your responses in the enclosed envelope addressed to XYZ Consulting.]

Thank you in advance for taking the time to complete this questionnaire. Client satisfaction is very important to us and we value your comments.

Sincerely,

FIRM NAME

Lawyer Name

Enclosures

Client Satisfaction Survey
(Sample)

In general, how satisfied are you with the firm in the following areas?
(Please circle one number for each answer.)

	Low				High
Overall quality of service	1	2	3	4	5
Responding to your needs	1	2	3	4	5
Completing work in a timely manner	1	2	3	4	5
Communicating with you about work or timing	1	2	3	4	5
Keeping you informed about changes in law, new cases	1	2	3	4	5
Providing recommendations and solutions to business problems	1	2	3	4	5
Understanding your business	1	2	3	4	5
Demonstrating knowledge of your industry	1	2	3	4	5
Competence of firm personnel (lawyers and staff)	1	2	3	4	5
Professionalism of personnel (lawyers and staff)	1	2	3	4	5
Firm billing practices	1	2	3	4	5
Informing you of other ways firm can assist you	1	2	3	4	5
Accessibility of firm personnel (lawyers and staff)	1	2	3	4	5

Do you read the firm's newsletter(s)? ❏ Yes ❏ No

    If yes, how satisfied are you with newsletter? 1 2 3 4 5

What do you like best about working with our firm?

_____

_____

What would you like to see our firm do better?

_____

_____

Have we ever asked you to recommend us to others? ❏ Yes ❏ No

    If not, would you refer the firm to someone who asks? ❏ Yes ❏ No

    If not, why not? _____

CHAPTER

1

LETTERS FOR
LAWYERS
Essential
Communications
for Clients,
Prospects, and
Others

Please check which of the firm's legal services we provide to you now, or have provided to you in the past:

- ❏ General Business Corporate
- ❏ Intellectual Property
- ❏ Corporate Governance
- ❏ Labor and Employment
- ❏ Employee Benefits
- ❏ Litigation
- ❏ Energy/Utilities

- ❏ Real Estate
- ❏ Environmental
- ❏ RICO/White Collar Crime
- ❏ Estate Planning/Wills/Trusts
- ❏ Other: _____
- ❏ Health Law

Please provide the names of other law firms you use, if any:

_____

_____

_____

Please specify your industry's main trade associations:

_____

_____

Is there anything else we could do to improve our service to you?
(If so, please identify.)

_____

_____

_____

_____

(Optional)
Your Name:_____

Company Name: _____

Would you like us to contact you about any of the above?   ❏ Yes   ❏ No

THANK YOU FOR YOUR PARTICIPATION!

Client Satisfaction Survey–
Pre-Survey Letter

FIELD {Date}

FIELD {Name}
FIELD {Company Name}
FIELD {Address}
FIELD {City, State, Zip Code}

Dear FIELD {Salutation}:

You are a valued client. It is important that our services to you are timely, responsive, and cost-effective. Our firm prides itself on the quality of legal services that we provide to our clients, and we want to know if there are any problems or if there is dissatisfaction with us at any level.

Accordingly, in the next week or so, [I OR the firm] will be sending you a Client Satisfaction Survey. [Please take the few minutes necessary to fill out the survey OR The survey will take approximately 20 minutes of your time.] Your time is very valuable, but your responses will help us to provide you and all of our clients with the best possible legal services.

Thank you in advance for your assistance.

Sincerely,

FIRM NAME

Lawyer Name

CHAPTER

1

LETTERS FOR
LAWYERS
Essential
Communications
for Clients,
Prospects, and
Others

Client Service Comment Form–
Cover Letter

FIELD {Date}

FIELD {Name}
FIELD {Company Name}
FIELD {Address}
FIELD {City, State, Zip Code}

Dear FIELD {Salutation}:

[Periodically OR At the conclusion of a matter], it is our custom to ask our
clients how we [are doing OR did]. Would you please take a few moments to
fill out the enclosed Client Service Comment Form and return it to us in the
enclosed self-addressed, stamped envelope?

Thank you for your time and assistance in ensuring that (Firm Name)
continues to provide and maintain the highest-quality legal services.

Sincerely,

FIRM NAME

Lawyer Name

Client Service Comment Form

	Poor	Fair	Good	Excellent
Overall quality of service				
Personnel (easy to work with, pleasant)				
Responsiveness (telephone calls, answering questions, etc.)				
Timeliness (meeting deadlines)				
Providing helpful recommendations				
Quality of legal product				

Please make recommendations on how we can improve our service to you:

_____

_____

General comments:

_____

_____

What additional services would help you?

_____

_____

Would you like us to call you regarding any of the above information?

❏ Yes   ❏ No

(Optional)

Name _____ Date _____

Company_____

Services provided _____

*Please complete this form and return it to us in the enclosed stamped envelope.
Thank you for your assistance.*

CHAPTER

1

LETTERS FOR
LAWYERS
Essential
Communications
for Clients,
Prospects, and
Others

Client Satisfaction Survey–
Post-Survey Thank You

FIELD {Date}

FIELD {Name}
FIELD {Company Name}
FIELD {Address}
FIELD {City, State, Zip Code}

Dear FIELD {Salutation}:

Thank you for taking the time to respond to our Client Satisfaction Survey. Your responses [and comments (if applicable)] were very helpful and appreciated. (If applicable) [Someone OR (identify who)] will be in touch with you shortly to discuss your comments.

Again, thank you for your participation.

Sincerely,

FIRM NAME

Managing Partner

Collection Letter No. I
(Phase 1)

FIELD {Date}

FIELD {Name}
FIELD {Company Name}
FIELD {Address}
FIELD {City, State, Zip Code}

Dear FIELD {Salutation}:

A review of your account indicates that the balance of $_____ is more than 30 days past due. In today's hectic world, many of us appreciate a reminder when our accounts are past due.

A copy of your invoice is enclosed, along with a stamped, self-addressed envelope. The firm would appreciate receiving your payment at your earliest convenience. If you have already mailed us a check, we thank you.

Sincerely,

FIRM NAME

Accounting Supervisor Name

Enclosures

CHAPTER

1

LETTERS FOR
LAWYERS
Essential
Communications
for Clients,
Prospects, and
Others

Collection Letter No. 2
(Phase 2)

FIELD {Date}

FIELD {Name}
FIELD {Company Name}
FIELD {Address}
FIELD {City, State, Zip Code}

Dear FIELD {Salutation}:

Our records indicate that your account [is over 60 days past due OR shows
that $_____ is 60 days past due and $_____ is over 30 days past due]. The
current balance due on your account is $_____. A copy of your most recent
invoice is enclosed. The firm would appreciate receiving your payment at
your earliest convenience. If you would like to discuss alternate payment
arrangements, please call me at (telephone number).

If you have already mailed us a check, we thank you.

Sincerely,

FIRM NAME

Accounting Supervisor Name

Enclosure

Collection Letter No. 3
(Phase 3)

FIELD {Date}

FIELD {Name}
FIELD {Company Name}
FIELD {Address}
FIELD {City, State, Zip Code}

Dear FIELD {Salutation}:

This is one of those letters that I do not like writing and I know that you cannot enjoy receiving. I am referring to the fact that your account [has fallen more than 90 days past due OR shows that $_____ is more than 90 days past due, $ _____ more than 60 days and $_____ more than 30 days past due]. We would like for you to remain a client of the firm and are anxious to mark your account current. Please attend to this matter by sending a check today. Enclosed is a copy of your latest invoice which shows that your account has a total balance due of $_____.

As was mutually agreed in our engagement letter, the firm will withdraw from representing [you OR your company] unless suitable arrangements are made to bring your account up to date. Accordingly, if I have not received your payment by (date) or other acceptable arrangements have not been made, the firm will no longer represent you in this matter.

If you are not able to send payment today or if you have a question, please call me at (telephone number). Thank you.

Sincerely,

FIRM NAME

Accounting Supervisor Name

Enclosures
cc: (Lawyer)

CHAPTER

1

LETTERS FOR
LAWYERS
Essential
Communications
for Clients,
Prospects, and
Others

Condolences

FIELD {Date}

FIELD {Name}
FIELD {Company Name}
FIELD {Address}
FIELD {City, State, Zip Code}

Dear FIELD {Salutation}:

With genuine sadness I learned of your [husband's OR wife's OR (other's)] passing. Please accept my [heartfelt OR sincere] sympathy on the loss of (name).

(Personal paragraph about the deceased)

[Example: "I met John sixteen years ago when I joined the firm. As a friend and an associate, John earned the respect of many OR (other personal comment)."]

[Example: "John had the respect and admiration of all of his colleagues. His cheerful disposition was an inspiration to all of us. He will be greatly missed by everyone here at (Firm Name)."]

If there is anything that I OR (Firm Name) can do to be of assistance during this difficult time, please let me know.

Sincerely,

Lawyer Name

Confirm or Change Meeting

FIELD {Date}

FIELD {Name}
FIELD {Company Name}
FIELD {Address}
FIELD {City, State, Zip Code}

Dear FIELD {Salutation}:

This letter will confirm [that our meeting previously scheduled for (day/date/time) has been rescheduled to (day/date/time) OR our meeting scheduled for (day/date/time)] at [your office OR our office].

I [understand the need to reschedule the meeting OR hope this has not caused you an inconvenience]. We look forward to meeting with you on (specify date).

Sincerely,

FIRM NAME

Lawyer Name

CHAPTER

1

LETTERS FOR
LAWYERS
Essential
Communications
for Clients,
Prospects, and
Others

Confirm Seminar Reservation

FIELD {Date}

FIELD {Name}
FIELD {Company Name}
FIELD {Address}
FIELD {City, State, Zip Code}

Dear FIELD {Salutation}:

Thank you for [reserving a seat at OR your check in the amount of (specify) as payment for] our seminar entitled "(title)." The seminar is scheduled on (day/date/time) at (location).

Registration begins at (time) and the program will start promptly at (time). We look forward to seeing you on (date).

Sincerely,

FIRM NAME

Lawyer Name

Congratulations
(Award)

FIELD {Date}

FIELD {Name}
FIELD {Company Name}
FIELD {Address}
FIELD {City, State, Zip Code}

Dear FIELD {Salutation}:

Congratulations on receiving the (blank) award in recognition for your [service OR contribution] to (name of organization). This well-deserved tribute is surely the result of your long and dedicated service. Certainly, all those associated with you in your efforts have benefited immensely. Great job!

[(Enclose copy of newspaper article, if applicable) OR I saw the article about your award in (identify publication) OR I heard about your award from (person's name)].

Again, congratulations on receiving this prestigious award.

Sincerely,

FIRM NAME

Lawyer Name

(Enclosure)

CHAPTER

1

LETTERS FOR
LAWYERS
Essential
Communications
for Clients,
Prospects, and
Others

Congratulations
(Birth of Child)

FIELD {Date}

FIELD {Name}
FIELD {Company Name}
FIELD {Address}
FIELD {City, State, Zip Code}

Dear FIELD {Salutation}:

Congratulations on the birth of your [daughter OR son]! With this wonderful addition, we know that the years ahead will be bright and happy ones for everyone in your family.

On behalf of all of us at (Firm Name), I extend best wishes to you, your [wife OR husband], and baby (baby's name).

Sincerely,

FIRM NAME

Lawyer Name

Congratulations

(New Position or Promotion)

FIELD {Date}

FIELD {Name}
FIELD {Company Name}
FIELD {Address}
FIELD {City, State, Zip Code}

Dear FIELD {Salutation}:

Congratulations on being [elected OR appointed OR promoted] to (name of position). You have worked hard to earn the recognition you presently enjoy at (name of organization), and they have made a wise choice in selecting you for this position. I know the organization will benefit from your strong leadership.

[(Enclose copy of newspaper article, if applicable) OR I saw the announcement in (identify publication) OR I heard about your recent achievement from (person's name)].

Please accept my heartiest congratulations on your [election OR appointment OR promotion] and my very best wishes for continued success.

Sincerely,

FIRM NAME

Lawyer Name

(Enclosure)

CHAPTER

1

LETTERS FOR
LAWYERS
Essential
Communications
for Clients,
Prospects, and
Others

Congratulations
(Office Move or Expansion)

FIELD {Date}

FIELD {Name}
FIELD {Company Name}
FIELD {Address}
FIELD {City, State, Zip Code}

Dear FIELD {Salutation}:

Congratulations on [your move to new offices OR the expansion of your firm]!

While moves are never easy, it is always exciting to find oneself in [new OR more spacious] surroundings. We at (Firm Name) are always elated when we see [our clients OR good friends] succeed. It is obvious that your success is directly attributable to strong leadership and solid management.

Again, congratulations and best wishes for continued success.

Sincerely,

FIRM NAME

Lawyer Name

End of Matter Confirmation Letter

FIELD {Date}

FIELD {Name}
FIELD {Company Name}
FIELD {Address}
FIELD {City, State, Zip Code}

Dear FIELD {Salutation}:

It was a pleasure to serve you in the recent (describe transaction or case for which the client was represented). This letter will confirm that the matter has been concluded, and any new representation will require a new engagement letter detailing what such representation will entail.

Now that the matter has concluded, (FIRM NAME) would like to hear from you about the services we provided you. Your responses to the attached End of Matter Questionnaire will help us ensure that the quality and efficiency of our legal services are the best possible.

Thank you again for allowing my firm to serve your legal needs. I look forward to the opportunity to provide additional services in the future. Again, your comments relating to the services you received will be helpful to us.

Sincerely,

FIRM NAME

Lawyer Name

Enclosure

CHAPTER

1

LETTERS FOR
LAWYERS
Essential
Communications
for Clients,
Prospects, and
Others

End of Matter Questionnaire

CLIENT NAME: _____ MATTER: _____

Please take a few minutes to answer the questions below. **Please *only* refer to the matter referenced above** in this particular evaluation. Please circle the appropriate number (ranging from 5 = Excellent to 1 = Poor) and provide any comments you wish to share with us. Thank you.

	Excellent				Poor
How would you rate the legal expertise of the lawyers assigned to this matter?	5	4	3	2	1
How responsive were our lawyers to your schedule in this matter?	5	4	3	2	1
How well were you treated by the lawyers and staff members who worked with you?	5	4	3	2	1
How well did we keep you informed of the status of this matter?	5	4	3	2	1
How satisfied are you with the result the firm obtained in this matter?	5	4	3	2	1
How would you rate the *value* of the legal services you received?	5	4	3	2	1
How satisfied are you with the overall performance of the firm?	5	4	3	2	1

Do you have any other comments?

Would you like someone to call you about this evaluation? ☐ Yes ☐ No

Please mail to: (Name)
(Address)
(City, State, Zip Code)

End of Matter Questionnaire
Cover Letter

FIELD {Date}

FIELD {Name}
FIELD {Company Name}
FIELD {Address}
FIELD {City, State, Zip Code}

Dear FIELD {Salutation}:

It was a pleasure to serve you in the recent (describe transaction or case for which the client was represented).

Now that the matter has concluded, (FIRM NAME) would like to hear from you about the services we provided you. Your responses to the attached End of Matter Questionnaire will help us ensure that the quality and efficiency of our legal services are the best possible.

Thank you again for the opportunity to be of service. I look forward to receiving your responses to the questionnaire.

Sincerely,

FIRM NAME

Lawyer Name

Enclosure

CHAPTER

1

LETTERS FOR
LAWYERS
Essential
Communications
for Clients,
Prospects, and
Others

Engagement Letter–
Follow-up Reminder Letter

FIELD {Date}

FIELD {Name}
FIELD {Company Name}
FIELD {Address}
FIELD {City, State, Zip Code}

Dear FIELD {Salutation}:

This letter is intended as a reminder that the firm still has not received your signed copy of our engagement letter [or the retainer fee (if applicable) in the amount of $_____].

In order to complete the process of opening your file for the representation detailed in our engagement, we must receive a signed copy. Enclosed is another copy of the letter in case you have misplaced the one previously sent. [(If applicable) Also, please include your retainer fee of $_____ with your letter.]

A self-addressed, stamped envelope is enclosed for your convenience in returning the letter. If you have any questions, please do not hesitate to call me.

Thank you for your assistance.

Sincerely,

FIRM NAME

Secretary Name

Enclosures
cc: (Lawyer)

Engagement Letter–New Client*

FIELD {Date}

FIELD {Name}
FIELD {Company Name}
FIELD {Address}
FIELD {City, State, Zip Code}

Dear FIELD {Salutation}:

I want to take this opportunity to personally thank you for selecting [me OR our firm] to represent you in (specify in detail what firm will do for client).

The fee arrangement, as agreed, will be based on [an hourly rate OR a fixed fee in the amount of $___ OR a contingency fee (specify %) OR (specify other)]. (If appropriate, indicate whether a retainer and the amount is required up front.) [(If hourly rate) Our hourly rates range from $___ to $___, depending on the experience level of the attorney or paralegal OR Our partners' rates range from $___ to $___; associates range from $___ to $___; and paralegals range from $___ to $___, depending on their respective level of experience OR (Partner A) bills at $___ per hour, (Associate B) bills at $___ per hour, and (Paralegal C) bills at $___ per hour.]

The firm bills on a monthly basis for any disbursements and any fees due. Disbursements include: (identify, e.g., photocopying, long distance charges, courier services, computer online services, court costs, travel, etc.). Payment is due upon receipt of our invoice. Failure to make timely payments may, upon notice, result in the firm's withdrawal as your counsel in this matter.

[I will be the only attorney working on your matter OR The members of the team that will be working on your matter include (Partner A), (Associate B), (Paralegal C), and (Secretary D).] Please feel free to call any member of our group for assistance.

Again, thank you for this opportunity to be of service. Please sign and return a copy of this letter in the enclosed self-addressed, stamped envelope. If you have any questions, please call me at (telephone number).

Sincerely,
FIRM NAME

ACKNOWLEDGED and Agreed to:

_____   Lawyer Name
Client Name

* **Caveat:** This letter is an example only. You should check your state's Code of Professional Responsibility for specific requirements regarding engagement letters.

CHAPTER

1

LETTERS FOR
LAWYERS
Essential
Communications
for Clients,
Prospects, and
Others

Engagement Letter–New Matter

FIELD {Date}

FIELD {Name}
FIELD {Company Name}
FIELD {Address}
FIELD {City, State, Zip Code}

Dear FIELD {Salutation}:

This letter confirms our [telephone conversation OR meeting] in which we agreed that the firm will represent you in (specify matter). We appreciate your continued trust and confidence in (FIRM NAME), and we will do our utmost to continue to earn it.

As we discussed, the firm will handle this matter [using our normal fee structure OR for the fixed fee of $_____ OR based on a contingency fee of ___ percent OR (specify other)]. All other aspects of our most current engagement letter will remain in effect.

Again, we appreciate the opportunity to be of service to (company).

Sincerely,

FIRM NAME

Lawyer Name

Firing a Client

FIELD {Date}

FIELD {Name}
FIELD {Company Name}
FIELD {Address}
FIELD {City, State, Zip Code}

Dear FIELD {Salutation}:

We appreciate the opportunity to have served as your law firm (state period of time). However, due to the circumstances surrounding (explain situation), we believe it is in the best interest of all concerned for you to seek other counsel to serve your needs. Therefore, it is with regret that we must terminate our representation of [you OR your company] at this time.

As a reminder, listed below are some of your upcoming deadlines which your new counsel will need to address: (State deadlines)

We will be glad to assist you and your new law firm in making this transition as smooth as possible.

Sincerely,

FIRM NAME

Lawyer Name

CHAPTER

1

LETTERS FOR
LAWYERS
Essential
Communications
for Clients,
Prospects, and
Others

Firm Name Change Letter to Clients

FIELD {Date}

FIELD {Name}
FIELD {Company Name}
FIELD {Address}
FIELD {City, State, Zip Code}

Dear FIELD {Salutation}:

As our new letterhead indicates, we have recently changed the name of our firm. (State reason for the change.)

While we may have changed our name, there is no change in our commitment to providing quality legal services to our clients. Enclosed is a new firm [brochure OR résumé] which outlines the legal services we provide to clients such as you.

Please let me know if I can provide additional information about the other services we do not currently provide you.

Sincerely,

FIRM NAME

Lawyer Name

Enclosure

Follow-up No. I
(After Convention or Event)

FIELD {Date}

FIELD {Name}
FIELD {Company Name}
FIELD {Address}
FIELD {City, State, Zip Code}

Dear FIELD {Salutation}:

It was great [seeing you OR meeting you OR running into you again] at the (name of conference/event/occasion) last week in (location). I hope you found it as rewarding as I did.

Enclosed are the materials [you requested OR I promised to send along]. They explain the legal services [I provide OR my firm provides] to clients. What you might find of particular interest is the information pertaining to (specify area of materials that addresses subject of inquiry OR conversation held).

I will call you next week to answer any questions you may have.

Again, it was good to [see OR meet] you in (location).

Sincerely,

FIRM NAME

Lawyer Name

Enclosure(s)

CHAPTER

1

LETTERS FOR
LAWYERS
Essential
Communications
for Clients,
Prospects, and
Others

Follow-up No. 2
(After Initial Meeting)

FIELD {Date}

FIELD {Name}
FIELD {Company Name}
FIELD {Address}
FIELD {City, State, Zip Code}

Dear FIELD {Salutation}:

I enjoyed [talking OR meeting] with you [today OR yesterday OR last week] at (specify place or occasion). Thank you for giving me the opportunity to discuss the legal services [I offer OR my firm offers].

Enclosed [are materials about my firm OR is a firm brochure OR is the information I promised I would forward to you]. You may find the information related to (specify) of particular interest.

I will call next week to follow up. In the meantime, please call me if you have any questions.

Sincerely,

FIRM NAME

Lawyer Name

Enclosure(s)

Follow-up No. 3
(After Seminar)

FIELD {Date}

FIELD {Name}
FIELD {Company Name}
FIELD {Address}
FIELD {City, State, Zip Code}

Dear FIELD {Salutation}:

It was great [seeing you OR meeting you] at the (mention seminar title) seminar [sponsored OR co-sponsored] by my firm. I hope you found the seminar helpful and that you find the materials distributed useful as you review the issues addressed during the session(s).

If you have any questions about the issues addressed at the seminar, or any other matters where we might provide assistance, please let me know.

Again, I am glad that you were able to be with us on (date).

Best wishes for continued success.

                    Sincerely,

                    FIRM NAME

                    Lawyer Name

CHAPTER

1

LETTERS FOR
LAWYERS
Essential
Communications
for Clients,
Prospects, and
Others

Follow-up No. 4
(After Telephone Call)

FIELD {Date}

FIELD {Name}
FIELD {Company Name}
FIELD {Address}
FIELD {City, State, Zip Code}

Dear FIELD {Salutation}:

Thank you for your call today. I enjoyed talking with you about (subject matter).

Enclosed [is a listing of legal services my firm offers clients OR is a firm brochure OR are materials about services provided by my firm in the area of (specify)].

Please let me know if I can provide additional information. I will call you next week to follow up.

Sincerely,

FIRM NAME

Lawyer Name

Enclosure(s)

Follow-up No. 5
(At Conclusion of Matter)

FIELD {Date}

FIELD {Name}
FIELD {Company Name}
FIELD {Address}
FIELD {City, State, Zip Code}

Dear FIELD {Salutation}:

Thank you for allowing [me OR (FIRM NAME)] to serve your legal needs in (matter).

It is my sincere hope that you are completely satisfied with the service you received and will avail yourself of our expertise in the future. The firm, in addition to (specify legal service provided), also provides services in other areas, such as (identify other practice areas).

We are always interested in suggestions that help us to improve our service. If you have not had a chance to return the Client Service Comment Form we sent to you earlier, I hope you will take a few moments to pass along your comments on the quality of the service you received from our firm.

Again, thank you for the opportunity to be of service.

Sincerely,

FIRM NAME

Lawyer Name

CHAPTER

1

LETTERS FOR
LAWYERS
Essential
Communications
for Clients,
Prospects, and
Others

Follow-up No. 6
(Lost Client)

FIELD {Date}

FIELD {Name}
FIELD {Company Name}
FIELD {Address}
FIELD {City, State, Zip Code}

Dear FIELD {Salutation}:

We regret that you have chosen another law firm to serve your legal needs. However, we appreciate the opportunity to have been of service to you, and we wish you well in the future.

Of course, we will cooperate fully with you and your new legal counsel during this transition period. We would appreciate your payment of all invoices due at the time you or your representative picks up your files.

If you have any questions now or in the future, please do not hesitate to call me personally.

Sincerely,

FIRM NAME

Lawyer Name

Holiday Greeting Letter –
Holiday Season

FIELD {Date}

FIELD {Name}
FIELD {Company Name}
FIELD {Address}
FIELD {City, State, Zip Code}

Dear FIELD {Salutation}:

On behalf of (FIRM NAME), I extend our very best wishes for a Happy Holiday Season and a prosperous New Year!

The holiday season gives us the opportunity to extend our personal thanks to our clients and acquaintances, and to offer our best wishes for 20XX. Our relationship is very important to me and to everyone at the firm.

Thanks again for a wonderful year.

HAPPY HOLIDAYS!

Sincerely,

FIRM NAME

Lawyer Name

CHAPTER

1

**LETTERS FOR
LAWYERS**
Essential
Communications
for Clients,
Prospects, and
Others

Holiday Greeting Letter –
Thanksgiving

FIELD {Date}

FIELD {Name}
FIELD {Company Name}
FIELD {Address}
FIELD {City, State, Zip Code}

Dear FIELD {Salutation}:

As the Thanksgiving holiday approaches, it affords us the opportunity to thank all our clients and friends for the many blessings they have given us.

We are most grateful for the confidence you have shown in (FIRM NAME) and thankful for [your business OR the referral you made]. Our firm values highly our many wonderful relationships, and we are happy to include people like you in that category.

Happy Thanksgiving!!

Sincerely,

FIRM NAME

Lawyer Name

Holiday Greeting Letter – Donation to Charity

FIELD {Date}

FIELD {Name}
FIELD {Company Name}
FIELD {Address}
FIELD {City, State, Zip Code}

Dear FIELD {Salutation}:

I want to take this opportunity to wish you a Happy Holiday Season, and a healthy and prosperous New Year.

(FIRM NAME) has made contributions to various charities in the name of our clients and friends. We feel so blessed and fortunate this holiday season that we thought we would extend a helping hand in the form of a monetary contribution to some of the organizations that serve those in our community that are in need.

The charities include:

[NAME OF CHARITIES THAT FIRM SENT CONTRIBUTION TO]

Best wishes to you, your family and colleagues this holiday season.

Sincerely,

FIRM NAME

Lawyer Name

CHAPTER

1

LETTERS FOR
LAWYERS
Essential
Communications
for Clients,
Prospects, and
Others

In-Person Client Interview –
Pre-Interview Letter No. 1

FIELD {Date}

FIELD {Name}
FIELD {Company Name}
FIELD {Address}
FIELD {City, State, Zip Code}

Dear FIELD {Salutation}:

As I recently discussed with you, our firm has instituted a practice of interviewing our clients to determine how we can improve our legal services. We value our longstanding relationship with (XYZ Company), and thought it would be helpful for our managing partner, (Name), [and (if appropriate) our director of client services, (Name),] to meet with you as part of that program to discuss our firm's services to you.

Accordingly, in the next week, I have asked (Name of person) from our office to call and schedule an in-person interview in your office. The interview will only take 30-45 minutes of your time.

Thank you for assisting with our efforts to better serve (XYZ Company). If you have any questions, please call me at (Telephone No.).

Sincerely,

FIRM NAME

Responsible/Billing Attorney Name

Cc: Managing Partner
    Marketing Director

In-Person Client Interview –
Pre-Interview Letter No. 2

FIELD {Date}

FIELD {Name}
FIELD {Company Name}
FIELD {Address}
FIELD {City, State, Zip Code}

Dear FIELD {Salutation}:

As a valued client, we want to learn from you. Specifically, we would like to [hear your views about the legal services provided by (FIRM NAME) OR discuss your expectations of your outside law firms that provide you legal services]. We know that clients want timely, responsive and cost-effective legal services, but we want to hear specifics from you.

With that in mind, our [director of client services, (name), OR (name other person),] will call you next week to set up a short meeting of 30-45 minutes with the firm's managing partner, (name), to discuss (FIRM NAME) in more detail.

Thank you in advance for your assistance as we try to become a better legal services provider.

Sincerely,

FIRM NAME

Responsible/Billing Attorney Name

Cc: Managing Partner
    Marketing Director

CHAPTER

1

LETTERS FOR
LAWYERS
Essential
Communications
for Clients,
Prospects, and
Others

In-Person Client Interview –
Pre-Interview Letter No. 3
(Client Services Director/Managing Partner)

FIELD {Date}

FIELD {Name}
FIELD {Company Name}
FIELD {Address}
FIELD {City, State, Zip Code}

Dear FIELD {Salutation}:

This will confirm our telephone conversation today.

Thank you for agreeing to see [me OR me and (name)] on (date) at (time) in your office. I appreciate your taking time out of your busy schedule to discuss (FIRM NAME) and the services we provide to you.

The following is a list of questions that we could cover. However, they are only intended as suggestions, and the conversation can cover whatever you wish to discuss. The suggested questions are:

- What is the overall satisfaction with (FIRM NAME)?
- Are you pleased with the legal services provided you?
- Specifically, how are we doing in the following areas:
    - Avoiding surprises?
    - Meeting deadlines?
    - Billing process?
    - Communicating often?
    - Work product?
    - Would you recommend our firm to others and, if so, why?

If you have any questions prior to our meeting, please do not hesitate to call me at (telephone number).

Sincerely,

FIRM NAME

Director of Client Services OR
Managing Partner

In-Person Client Interview –
Post-Interview Letter

FIELD {Date}

FIELD {Name}
FIELD {Company Name}
FIELD {Address}
FIELD {City, State, Zip Code}

Dear FIELD {Salutation}:

Thank you visiting with [me OR (name) and me] on (date) at (time) in your office. I/We are most grateful to you for taking the time to meet with me/us to discuss your relationship with (FIRM NAME).

[Where applicable:
We are always delighted to hear that the attorneys and staff of (FIRM NAME) are providing quality services and that our clients are pleased with our firm. We also recognize that we can always improve the services we provide, and I assure you that we will endeavor to do that.

OR

We are grateful to learn that there are areas in which we can improve our services. Those areas you specifically mentioned will be addressed immediately, and we will advise you on the actions the firm [takes OR will take] to improve our services and procedures.]

Thanks again for seeing us, and for sharing your views.

Sincerely,

FIRM NAME

Managing Partner

CHAPTER

1

**LETTERS FOR
LAWYERS**
Essential
Communications
for Clients,
Prospects, and
Others

Lawyer/Paralegal Assignment Change

FIELD {Date}

FIELD {Name}
FIELD {Company Name}
FIELD {Address}
FIELD {City, State, Zip Code}

Dear FIELD {Salutation}:

It was a pleasure [talking OR meeting] with you today.

As I [mentioned OR mentioned on the telephone], [(Lawyer Name) OR (Paralegal Name)] will [replace (Lawyer/Paralegal Name) on OR be added to the team handling] (specify matter) for [you OR your company] due to (state reason).

Be assured that (Lawyer/Paralegal Name) will do an excellent job on your matter. (State something positive about Lawyer or Paralegal.)

Sincerely,

FIRM NAME

Lawyer Name

Lawyer Unavailable

FIELD {Date}

FIELD {Name}
FIELD {Company Name}
FIELD {Address}
FIELD {City, State, Zip Code}

Dear FIELD {Salutation}:

Thank you for your letter dated (date). (Lawyer Name) is out of the office [for a trial OR on vacation OR (other reason)]. He/She will be unavailable for (state time period). I will bring your letter to his/her attention immediately upon his/her return.

If I can be of any assistance during (Lawyer Name's) absence, please let me know.

Sincerely,

FIRM NAME

[Secretary OR
Paralegal for Lawyer Name]

CHAPTER

1

LETTERS FOR
LAWYERS
Essential
Communications
for Clients,
Prospects, and
Others

Merger Announcement No. 1
(Acquiring Firm)
(Send to Clients before Merger)

FIELD {Date}

FIELD {Name}
FIELD {Company Name}
FIELD {Address}
FIELD {City, State, Zip Code}

Dear FIELD {Salutation}:

The complexities of today's laws demand a high level of expertise in many different areas of the law. In order to continue to meet our clients' legal needs, it is important that our firm keep pace with this growing demand. With these challenges and opportunities in mind, we are pleased to announce that we will merge with (name of acquired firm), a well-respected, client-oriented law firm. This new association will be effective on (date).

When considering a merger, it was important that both firms share the same concerns and goals for client satisfaction and quality service. In addition, both firms possess the necessary knowledge and experience in [a wide range of practice areas OR specify practice areas].

As a client, you will notice [little change OR no change]. Our office location and telephone number [will remain the same OR give new information here]. I will continue to be your principal contact with the firm.

We are excited about this new association and about the opportunities to better meet your legal needs. We hope that our expanded resources, timeliness, and additional expertise will be beneficial to all of our clients.

We look forward to our continued relationship.

Sincerely,

FIRM NAME

Lawyer Name

Merger Announcement No. 2 (Acquired Firm)
(Send to Clients before Merger)

FIELD {Date}

FIELD {Name}
FIELD {Company Name}
FIELD {Address}
FIELD {City, State, Zip Code}

Dear FIELD {Salutation}:

In order to keep pace with the growing needs of our clients, it has become necessary for our firm to strengthen its resources to meet this demand. Because of the growing complexities of today's laws, a greater level of expertise is necessary to provide excellent legal services. With these challenges and opportunities in mind, we have chosen to merge with (name of new firm), a well-respected, client-oriented law firm. This new association will be effective on (date).

When considering the merger, it was important that both firms share the same concerns and goals for client satisfaction and quality service, as well as the necessary broad base of knowledge and experience in the many areas of the law. We are excited about this new association and about the opportunities to better serve your legal needs.

As a client, other than our new name, you will notice very little change. Our office location and telephone number [will remain the same OR give new information here]. As we transition to this new arrangement, you will continue to receive the prompt, professional service you have been accustomed to.

We look forward to continuing our relationship with you as (FIRM NAME).

Sincerely,

FIRM NAME

Lawyer Name

CHAPTER

1

LETTERS FOR
LAWYERS
Essential
Communications
for Clients,
Prospects, and
Others

Misunderstanding–Apology
(General)

FIELD {Date}

FIELD {Name}
FIELD {Company Name}
FIELD {Address}
FIELD {City, State, Zip Code}

Dear FIELD {Salutation}:

Please accept my apologies for the misunderstanding regarding (state problem). [As we discussed OR Accordingly], we will (state action to be taken regarding problem).

At (FIRM NAME), our attorneys take a personal interest in every client. Our goal is to provide our clients with timely and accurate work, especially when we experience frequent changes in pertinent laws and regulations. Regrettably, we do not reach these goals 100 percent of the time. Nonetheless, we will continue to work at improving the services we provide to you and all our clients.

As always, please feel free to call me at (phone number) with additional comments and suggestions.

Sincerely,

FIRM NAME

Lawyer Name

Misunderstanding–Apology
(Regarding Billing)

FIELD {Date}

FIELD {Name}
FIELD {Company Name}
FIELD {Address}
FIELD {City, State, Zip Code}

Dear FIELD {Salutation}:

Please accept my apologies for the misunderstanding regarding the services we provided to [you OR company name] and the corresponding fee [charges OR discrepancies] from (date to date). [As we discussed OR Accordingly], we (state the action that will be taken regarding the invoice). In order to prevent this situation from occurring again, this letter will clarify our billing and fee procedures.

Many professional service businesses are compensated for the services provided to clients by taking the time required to complete the work and multiplying it by the appropriate hourly rate. Our hourly rates range from (range of fees) per hour, depending on the lawyer's level of experience. Our policy is to assign responsibilities in the most cost-effective manner.

Our partners review "work in progress" for each client on an ongoing basis. We evaluate the need to contact a client regarding any unexpected problems we've encountered in our research, calculations, and other situations in which the time incurred on the project may be more than originally antici-pated. In [some OR most] cases, the additional unexpected time is added to the total engagement cost.

If you have any questions regarding our billing and engagement procedures, please call me at (phone number). Your business is valuable to us, and we hope that you will accept our apology for this misunderstanding. We look forward to continuing to serve your legal needs.

Sincerely,

FIRM NAME

Lawyer Name

CHAPTER

1

LETTERS FOR
LAWYERS
Essential
Communications
for Clients,
Prospects, and
Others

New Client Letter to Former Law Firm

FIELD {Date}

FIELD {Name}
FIELD {Company Name}
FIELD {Address}
FIELD {City, State, Zip Code}

Dear FIELD {Salutation}:

Although [we OR I] have enjoyed working with you in the past and have appreciated all your help, [we OR I] have decided to make a change and move [our OR my] legal work to (FIRM NAME).

Given this new situation, I hereby instruct you to release all [records OR files] concerning (Name of business) to (Name of new lawyer or firm). [We OR I] would appreciate your cooperation and assistance during this time of transition.

Thank you in advance for your cooperation.

Sincerely,

FIRM NAME

Client Name

New Client Welcome

FIELD {Date}

FIELD {Name}
FIELD {Company Name}
FIELD {Address}
FIELD {City, State, Zip Code}

Dear FIELD {Salutation}:

Thank you for choosing (FIRM NAME) to serve your legal needs. We look forward to working with you.

As you become better acquainted with our firm, you will find that our lawyers have extensive experience assisting clients in the area of (specify). Consequently, we have a thorough understanding of your specific needs and the many issues which may affect [you OR your business].

If, at any time, you have any recommendations regarding how we might better serve you, please contact me personally. On behalf of all the lawyers and staff of (FIRM NAME), welcome!

Sincerely,

FIRM NAME

[Lawyer Name OR
Managing Partner]

CHAPTER

1

LETTERS FOR
LAWYERS
Essential
Communications
for Clients,
Prospects, and
Others

Open House Invitation
(Letter Form)

FIELD {Date}

FIELD {Name}
FIELD {Company Name}
FIELD {Address}
FIELD {City, State, Zip Code}

Dear FIELD {Salutation}:

You're Invited!

This summer marks the (specify) anniversary of the move to our present location [or whatever the occasion may be for a celebration]. Many of you attended our Open House in 19XX. Over the years, our staff has increased, our offices have changed, and our clients and contacts have grown.

As a way of showing our appreciation to you and other friends of the firm, please join us at our Open House on Monday, December 3, 20XX, from 4:00 to 7:00 p.m. at our offices at 123 Main Street, Anytown, USA.

Please RSVP by (date) to (telephone number) [or return the enclosed card].

We look forward to seeing you on December 3!

Sincerely,

FIRM NAME

Lawyer Name

Open House Invitation Card No. 1
(General)

You Are Cordially Invited to Attend Our

[Client Appreciation OR (name reason)]

OPEN HOUSE

Monday, December 3, 20XX
4 - 7 p.m.
at
Whiteacre, Blackacre & Greenacre
123 Main Street
Anytown, USA

Please RSVP by (date) to
(Name of person and telephone number)
[or return the enclosed response card]

CHAPTER

1

LETTERS FOR
LAWYERS
Essential
Communications
for Clients,
Prospects, and
Others

Open House Invitation Card No. 2
(Holiday Event)

Whiteacre, Blackacre & Greenacre

Invites You to Attend a

Holiday Open House
[or Holiday Celebration]*

Monday, December 3, 20XX
4:00 - 7:00 p.m.
at
123 Main Street
Anytown, USA

*Donations of canned food will be accepted for the
Food Pantry Foundation House

Please RSVP by (date)
[to (contact person's name) at (telephone number)
or by returning the enclosed response card].

Partner Buy-Out Notification

FIELD {Date}

FIELD {Name}
FIELD {Company Name}
FIELD {Address}
FIELD {City, State, Zip Code}

Dear FIELD {Salutation}:

This is to inform you that [I have assumed (Lawyer Name)'s practice OR I have bought out my partner, (name)'s, interest in our law firm OR (Lawyer Name) has retired from the firm]. The firm will [operate OR continue to operate] under the name of (specify).

As one of [his OR the firm's] important clients, I wanted to let you know that the firm will continue to serve your legal interests with the same high-quality service which (Lawyer Name) has strived for years to render to his clients.

I wanted to take this opportunity to let you know about this change and to thank you for your trust and confidence in the firm in the past. I hope you will continue to rely upon (FIRM NAME) for your legal needs.

I will call you next week to set up an appointment at your convenience to [get acquainted OR discuss the (specify current legal matter being handled by firm) OR discuss your current and future legal needs]. In the meantime, if you have any questions, please call me at (telephone number).

Sincerely,

FIRM NAME

Lawyer Name

CHAPTER

1

LETTERS FOR
LAWYERS
Essential
Communications
for Clients,
Prospects, and
Others

Payment Delay Authorization

FIELD {Date}

FIELD {Name}
FIELD {Company Name}
FIELD {Address}
FIELD {City, State, Zip Code}

Dear FIELD {Salutation}:

Thank you for your [letter OR call] of (date) explaining the circumstances surrounding your request for an extension of time to pay your invoice in the amount of $_____.

We do appreciate your candor and have noted on your account that your payment will be made on (date).

You have been a [loyal OR good] client of ours for [a long time OR (specify period)], so we are happy to extend this courtesy to you at this time.

Sincerely,

FIRM NAME

Lawyer Name

Payment Plan Letter No. 1

FIELD {Date}

FIELD {Name}
FIELD {Company Name}
FIELD {Address}
FIELD {City, State, Zip Code}

Dear FIELD {Salutation}:

A review of your account indicates that we have not yet received your
monthly payment in the amount of $_____. If your payment is in the mail,
please disregard this reminder.

Many of us appreciate a reminder, given the hectic pace of our daily lives.
Please take a moment, if you have not already done so, to send us your
monthly payment today.

Again, if you have already sent us a check, we thank you.

Sincerely,

FIRM NAME

Accounting Supervisor Name

CHAPTER

1

LETTERS FOR
LAWYERS
Essential
Communications
for Clients,
Prospects, and
Others

Payment Plan Letter No. 2

FIELD {Date}

FIELD {Name}
FIELD {Company Name}
FIELD {Address}
FIELD {City, State, Zip Code}

Dear FIELD {Salutation}:

This is a reminder that the firm has still not received your monthly payment in the amount of $_____ for the past month. In addition, your (specify month) bill is also due at this time. Please forward a check today for both payments.

(FIRM NAME) makes an extra effort to work with our clients in facilitating the payment of their accounts. If there is a problem regarding the specific arrangements we have made with you, we would like to hear from you. If this is merely an oversight, it would be most appreciated if you could send your scheduled monthly payments today.

Thank you.

Sincerely,

FIRM NAME

Accounting Supervisor Name

Proposal Cover Letter

FIELD {Date}

FIELD {Name}
FIELD {Company Name}
FIELD {Address}
FIELD {City, State, Zip Code}

Dear FIELD {Salutation}:

Thank you for the opportunity to submit the enclosed ["Proposal for Legal Services" OR (specify name)].

I hope this information is responsive to your request. The work will be performed by the undersigned and (identify other team members, including secretaries and paralegals). We look forward to serving [you OR (specify company OR organization name)] in [resolving (specify legal problem) OR preparing (specify legal document or documents].

Please call me if you have any questions. I will contact you next week to follow up.

Sincerely,

FIRM NAME

Lawyer Name

Enclosure

CHAPTER

1

LETTERS FOR
LAWYERS
Essential
Communications
for Clients,
Prospects, and
Others

Rate Increase

(Send before Invoice)

FIELD {Date}

FIELD {Name}
FIELD {Company Name}
FIELD {Address}
FIELD {City, State, Zip Code}

Dear FIELD {Salutation}:

Thank you for giving us the opportunity to serve your legal needs in (state nature of matter).

Due to increased operating costs associated with operating our firm, it has become necessary for us to raise our rates effective [January 1 OR whenever]. Accordingly, the rates associated with your matter will be [$_____ per hour OR $_____ per hour for attorney A and $_____ for paralegal B].

If you have any questions, please contact me and I will discuss this matter with you further.

Sincerely,

FIRM NAME

Lawyer Name

Referral "Thank You" No. 1

FIELD {Date}

FIELD {Name}
FIELD {Company Name}
FIELD {Address}
FIELD {City, State, Zip Code}

Dear FIELD {Salutation}:

Thank you for referring [person OR company] to (FIRM NAME).

We [have met OR will meet] with (name) this week regarding [his/her OR their] legal needs. We look forward to providing [individual OR company name] with the finest and most cost-effective service possible.

Again, we appreciate your continued support and the confidence you have shown in us. I look forward to returning the favor at the earliest opportunity.

Sincerely,

FIRM NAME

Lawyer Name

CHAPTER

1

LETTERS FOR
LAWYERS
Essential
Communications
for Clients,
Prospects, and
Others

Referral "Thank You" No. 2

FIELD {Date}

FIELD {Name}
FIELD {Company Name}
FIELD {Address}
FIELD {City, State, Zip Code}

Dear FIELD {Salutation}:

Recently [individual OR company name] contacted [me OR our firm] to discuss [his/her OR their] needs for professional legal services. [He/She] mentioned that [you OR someone at your company] suggested (he/she) contact our firm. We sincerely appreciate this recommendation and referral. We will do our best to provide [individual OR company name] with the finest possible service.

Again, we are very grateful for the referral. I will reciprocate at the earliest opportunity.

Best regards,

FIRM NAME

Lawyer Name

Referral "Thank You" No. 3

FIELD {Date}

FIELD {Name}
FIELD {Company Name}
FIELD {Address}
FIELD {City, State, Zip Code}

Dear FIELD {Salutation}:

Thank you for recommending (FIRM NAME) to [individual OR company name]. We hope that we will have the opportunity to work with [him/her OR them] in the near future.

We recognize the faith you have placed in us by this referral. I assure you that we will make every effort to provide [name of person OR business] with the best possible legal services.

Once again, we appreciate the confidence you have placed in us. Thank you, and I hope I will have the opportunity to reciprocate in the near future.

Best regards,

FIRM NAME

Lawyer Name

CHAPTER

1

LETTERS FOR LAWYERS
Essential
Communications
for Clients,
Prospects, and
Others

Referral "Thank You" No. 4

FIELD {Date}

FIELD {Name}
FIELD {Company Name}
FIELD {Address}
FIELD {City, State, Zip Code}

Dear FIELD {Salutation}:

(Name of Client) has retained [me OR our firm] to represent [him/her OR his/her company]. [I OR We] look forward to working together with [individual OR company name] in meeting [his/her OR their] legal needs.

During our initial conference, [he OR she] informed me that we were selected based on your recommendation. I want to thank you for this referral. In our fast-paced society, we sometimes forget to thank those responsible for our continued growth. Your recommendation of our firm demonstrates the trust you have placed in us. We will do whatever we can to provide (name) with exceptional legal assistance and to preserve the trust you have placed in us.

Again, we appreciate the referral and your continued support.

Best regards,

FIRM NAME

Lawyer Name

Regret Client Employee Resignation

FIELD {Date}

FIELD {Name}
FIELD {Company Name}
FIELD {Address}
FIELD {City, State, Zip Code}

Dear FIELD {Salutation}:

It is with [deep regret OR regret] that we learned of your [recent OR upcoming] resignation from (Client Company Name). On behalf of the partners of (FIRM NAME), we are sorry to hear the news. We have always enjoyed working with you and will miss you.

We recognize that change is part of everyday life and things do not stay the same. Nonetheless, we are sad to see you leave and wish you the very best in your [future endeavors OR new position]. If I or the firm can assist in any way during your time of transition, please let me know.

Please keep in touch. (If appropriate: If the firm can serve you in your new position, please call me.)

With our very best wishes, I am

Sincerely,

FIRM NAME

Lawyer Name

CHAPTER

1

LETTERS FOR
LAWYERS
Essential
Communications
for Clients,
Prospects, and
Others

Requesting Referrals No. 1
(After Completing Matter)

FIELD {Date}

FIELD {Name}
FIELD {Company Name}
FIELD {Address}
FIELD {City, State, Zip Code}

Dear FIELD {Salutation}:

Thank you for giving (FIRM NAME) the opportunity to serve you. We are confident that (specify work performed) will prove to be beneficial to you and your company.

(FIRM NAME) provides (specify services offered) services to a variety of clients in a number of different professions and industries. We take personal pride in helping our clients with their legal needs in an efficient and cost-effective manner.

If you know of anyone in need of legal services, we hope you will refer them to us. We would welcome the opportunity to discuss our services and, specifically, how we can help them with their legal needs.

Sincerely,

FIRM NAME

Lawyer Name

Requesting Referrals No. 2
(From Corporate Client)

FIELD {Date}

FIELD {Name}
FIELD {Company Name}
FIELD {Address}
FIELD {City, State, Zip Code}

Dear FIELD {Salutation}:

On behalf of everyone at (FIRM NAME), we would like to thank you for letting us serve your legal needs. We enjoy working with (name of contact(s)). [He/She is OR They are] extremely helpful in providing the assistance needed for us to render our service in a timely manner.

For your information, the attorneys at (FIRM NAME) have extensive experience working with clients in a wide variety of professions and industries. (Expand here on other practice areas, as appropriate.)

We hope that you will keep us in mind if you or any of your business associates or friends are in need of experienced legal counsel. We would be happy to be of assistance.

Again, we appreciate the opportunity to work with you and (company name). If you have any recommendations on how we could better serve you, please call me at (telephone number).

Sincerely,

FIRM NAME

Lawyer Name

CHAPTER

1

LETTERS FOR
LAWYERS
Essential
Communications
for Clients,
Prospects, and
Others

Requesting Referrals No. 3
(Expanding Client Base)

FIELD {Date}

FIELD {Name}
FIELD {Company Name}
FIELD {Address}
FIELD {City, State, Zip Code}

Dear FIELD {Salutation}:

On behalf of (FIRM NAME), we thank you for your [business OR patronage] and support. We value your business and hope we can continue to advise you and (name of firm) in the future. If you have suggestions on ways we could improve our service to you, I would appreciate hearing from you.

Currently, we are looking to expand our client base by adding [businesses OR individuals in (state type of client OR industry desired)]. We hope that you will keep (FIRM NAME) in mind if you know of anyone in need of legal counsel. We would be happy to explain our services and how we could be of assistance.

Again, we thank you for your business and continued support.

Sincerely,

FIRM NAME

Lawyer Name

Retainer Fee–
Reminder Letter No. 1

FIELD {Date}

FIELD {Name}
FIELD {Company Name}
FIELD {Address}
FIELD {City, State, Zip Code}

Dear FIELD {Salutation}:

A review of your file indicates that we have not yet received your retainer fee in the amount of $_____.

Many of us appreciate a reminder due to the hectic nature of our daily lives. Please take a moment, if you have not already done so, to send us your retainer check today. I have included a self-addressed, stamped envelope for your convenience. If you have already sent us a check, we thank you.

Sincerely,

FIRM NAME

Secretary Name

Enclosure

CHAPTER

1

LETTERS FOR
LAWYERS
Essential
Communications
for Clients,
Prospects, and
Others

Retainer Fee–
Reminder Letter No. 2

FIELD {Date}

FIELD {Name}
FIELD {Company Name}
FIELD {Address}
FIELD {City, State, Zip Code}

Dear FIELD {Salutation}:

This is a reminder that the firm still has not received your retainer check in the amount of $_____.

In order for us to continue representing you on the (specify) matter, your file must be current. If we do not receive your retainer within seven (7) days, we will assume that you are no longer interested in our continued representation of you in this matter. If this is the case, we will cease to work further on your matter and will bill you for time already spent on it.

We would like you to remain a client of the firm and are anxious to mark your account current. Please attend to this matter today. I have included a self-addressed, stamped envelope for your convenience. If you have already sent us a check, we thank you.

If you have any questions or are not able to send payment immediately, please call me at (telephone number) today. Thank you.

Sincerely,

FIRM NAME

[Secretary Name or
Lawyer Name]

Enclosure
cc: (Lawyer)

Retainer Fee–
Replenishment Letter No. 1

FIELD {Date}

FIELD {Name}
FIELD {Company Name}
FIELD {Address}
FIELD {City, State, Zip Code}

Dear FIELD {Salutation}:

This is to advise you that the amount of your retainer is now below
$_____. It is the firm's practice when retainers fall to this level to
request a payment to restore the retainer to its original level. Accordingly,
please send a check in the amount of $_____. I have included a
self-addressed, stamped envelope for your convenience.

The amount of the retainer and the current balance on your account will be
reflected in your next billing statement. If you have any questions, please
contact me at (telephone number).

Sincerely,

FIRM NAME

Accounting Supervisor Name

Enclosure

CHAPTER

1

LETTERS FOR
LAWYERS
Essential
Communications
for Clients,
Prospects, and
Others

Retainer Fee–
Replenishment Letter No. 2

FIELD {Date}

FIELD {Name}
FIELD {Company Name}
FIELD {Address}
FIELD {City, State, Zip Code}

Dear FIELD {Salutation}:

This is a reminder that the firm still has not received your check in the amount of $_____ to bring your retainer fee to its original amount. Many of us appreciate a reminder due to the hectic nature of our daily lives. Please take a moment, if you have not already done so, to send us your retainer check today.

I have included a self-addressed, stamped envelope for your convenience.

If you have any questions or are not able to send payment immediately, please call me at (telephone number) today. Thank you.

Sincerely,

FIRM NAME

Accounting Supervisor Name

Enclosure

Sending Item of Interest
(Article about Firm)

FIELD {Date}

FIELD {Name}
FIELD {Company Name}
FIELD {Address}
FIELD {City, State, Zip Code}

Dear FIELD {Salutation}:

The firm was very proud of the recent coverage it received in (name of publication). It is always gratifying to receive favorable coverage for [the efforts of one of our lawyers OR our efforts on behalf of our clients].

I have enclosed a copy of the article in case you missed it.

Sincerely,

FIRM NAME

Lawyer Name

Enclosure

CHAPTER

1

LETTERS FOR
LAWYERS
Essential
Communications
for Clients,
Prospects, and
Others

Sending Item of Interest
(Article Authored at Firm)

FIELD {Date}

FIELD {Name}
FIELD {Company Name}
FIELD {Address}
FIELD {City, State, Zip Code}

Dear FIELD {Salutation}:

[I OR (Lawyer Name), a partner/associate with the firm,] wrote the enclosed article, which appeared in (publication). It deals with [the very important subject of (specify) OR a very timely topic].

[I thought you might find the article interesting OR I thought I would send a copy of the article along to you, in case you missed it.]

Sincerely,

FIRM NAME

Lawyer Name

Enclosure

Sending Item of Interest
(General)

FIELD {Date}

FIELD {Name}
FIELD {Company Name}
FIELD {Address}
FIELD {City, State, Zip Code}

Dear FIELD {Salutation}:

Thought the enclosed [article OR item] on (subject) would be of interest to you.

Best wishes!

Sincerely,

FIRM NAME

Lawyer Name

Enclosure

Note: In the alternative, staple business card with brief, handwritten note to item and mail.

CHAPTER

1

LETTERS FOR
LAWYERS
Essential
Communications
for Clients,
Prospects, and
Others

Tax Time Reminder

FIELD {Date}

FIELD {Name}
FIELD {Company Name}
FIELD {Address}
FIELD {City, State, Zip Code}

Dear FIELD {Salutation}:

With tax season rapidly approaching, you will want to begin to gather the information needed for preparing your (tax year) federal and state income tax returns. For your convenience, a checklist is enclosed. You can use it to prepare information for your tax return preparer.

If you have any legal questions regarding this year's taxes, please call me.

Sincerely,

FIRM NAME

Lawyer Name

Enclosure

"Thank You" No. 1
(After Office or Facility Visit)

FIELD {Date}

FIELD {Name}
FIELD {Company Name}
FIELD {Address}
FIELD {City, State, Zip Code}

Dear FIELD {Salutation}:

I very much appreciated the opportunity to visit your [office OR plant OR facility at (specify location) OR (other)]. Please [accept my thanks for your hospitality OR extend my heartfelt thanks to (person's name)] for [the excellent tour OR (other courtesy)].

I was very impressed with your operation and can see why it runs so efficiently. I find that clients can be better served if I get to know their businesses better and become more familiar with their [offices OR facilities]. It makes my job easier and results in better, more efficient representation for clients.

Again, thank you for your hospitality [and for joining me at lunch OR for treating me to lunch (if applicable)].

Sincerely,

FIRM NAME

Lawyer Name

73

CHAPTER

1

LETTERS FOR
LAWYERS
Essential
Communications
for Clients,
Prospects, and
Others

"Thank You" No. 2
(For Complimenting Employee)

FIELD {Date}

FIELD {Name}
FIELD {Company Name}
FIELD {Address}
FIELD {City, State, Zip Code}

Dear FIELD {Salutation}:

Thank you for your kind letter regarding the excellent [service OR treatment] you received from one of our [employees OR staff members OR lawyers]. A copy of your letter has been forwarded to our [personnel OR human resources] department and will be included in (the person's name)'s file.

Although we expect everyone at (FIRM NAME) to treat our clients in this manner, it is seldom that someone takes the time to write a letter of appreciation. I want to let you know how much I appreciate it, as I am sure (employee's first name) does.

Again, on behalf of everyone at (FIRM NAME), thank you for writing.

Sincerely,

FIRM NAME

[Managing Partner or
Lawyer Name]

copy to: (employee's name)
          Personnel file

"Thank You" No. 3
(For a Kindness)

FIELD {Date}

FIELD {Name}
FIELD {Company Name}
FIELD {Address}
FIELD {City, State, Zip Code}

Dear FIELD {Salutation}:

Please accept [my OR our] sincere thanks for [your thoughtfulness OR your support OR your generosity OR other]. [I OR We] especially appreciated your [taking the time to show us the city OR taking us to dinner OR other personal comment]. [I OR We] hope that [I OR we] can reciprocate in the near future.

Looking forward to seeing you soon. Thank you, again.

Sincerely,

Lawyer Name

CHAPTER

1

LETTERS FOR
LAWYERS
Essential
Communications
for Clients,
Prospects, and
Others

"Thank You" No. 4
(Longstanding Relationship)

FIELD {Date}

FIELD {Name}
FIELD {Company Name}
FIELD {Address}
FIELD {City, State, Zip Code}

Dear FIELD {Salutation}:

Call it [nostalgia OR just plain sentiment], but I was looking over a list of our clients of several years and stopped when I arrived at [your name OR the name of your company].

It has been a long time since our first transaction together (specify date or year, if possible). With a great deal of pride, I reflect on how far both of our firms have come since that time. The fact that our relationship has not only lasted but flourished is most rewarding.

I wanted to let you know that we do not take that relationship for granted. Thank you for letting the firm serve your legal needs over these many years. We hope your trust in us will continue for many more [years OR decades].

Sincerely,

FIRM NAME

Lawyer Name

Unable to Reach by Telephone

FIELD {Date}

FIELD {Name}
FIELD {Company Name}
FIELD {Address}
FIELD {City, State, Zip Code}

Dear FIELD {Salutation}:

I am sorry that we have not been able to connect by phone. I know how hectic things can get at times. Please do not hesitate to call if I or my firm can be of assistance to you in any way.

(Consider sending item along.) Enclosed is an [article OR item] of possible interest to you.

Sincerely,

FIRM NAME

Lawyer Name

(Enclosure)

Communication with Employees and Prospective Employees

W ith the pressures associated with the practice of law today, it is sometimes difficult to attract and retain good employees. Lawyers not only must be skilled practitioners, they need to be effective personnel managers as well. Effective communication with the firm's employees and prospective employees will prevent unnecessary turnover and attract desirable employees to the firm.

In this chapter, you will find letters to recognize such important events as an employee's anniversary with the firm, a promotion, or the birth of a child. There are letters to employment candidates and various letters of congratulations. You will find an appropriate letter for every occasion – whether you are welcoming a new employee, providing a reference, acknowledging receipt of a résumé, or regretting an employee's resignation.

Effective written communications with employees is one additional means to ensure good management. The letters in this chapter can be a resource to help communicate more effectively with current staff and those potential employees who come in contact with your firm.

Anniversary Cover Letter

2

LETTERS FOR
LAWYERS
Essential
Communications
for Clients,
Prospects, and
Others

FIELD {Date}

FIELD {Name}
FIELD {Company Name}
FIELD {Address}
FIELD {City, State, Zip Code}

Dear FIELD {Salutation}:

(Date) will mark your (number of years) anniversary as an [attorney OR employee] of (Firm Name). On behalf of all of us at the firm, I would like to take this opportunity to thank you for these past (number of) years of service and for your dedication to the firm.

We know that the success of the firm is due, in a major way, to the strong and capable efforts of [attorneys OR staff members] such as yourself. Your contribution has helped us maintain the position we enjoy within the legal community.

Again, the [firm OR partnership] extends our congratulations on your (number) anniversary.

Sincerely,

FIRM NAME

Managing Partner

Candidate Who Declined Employment Offer

FIELD {Date}

FIELD {Name}
FIELD {Company Name}
FIELD {Address}
FIELD {City, State, Zip Code}

Dear FIELD {Salutation}:

Thank you for your recent [letter OR telephone call]. We were disappointed that you have decided not to join our firm. Your background and qualifications are impressive, and you will surely be successful at any firm.

I wanted to take this opportunity to congratulate you on your new position and to extend our best wishes for your continued success.

Sincerely,

FIRM NAME

Lawyer Name

CHAPTER

2

LETTERS FOR
LAWYERS
Essential
Communications
for Clients,
Prospects, and
Others

Congratulations–
Birth of Employee's Child

FIELD {Date}

FIELD {Name}
FIELD {Company Name}
FIELD {Address}
FIELD {City, State, Zip Code}

Dear FIELD {Salutation}:

Congratulations on the birth of your [daughter OR son]! (Baby's name) is fortunate to be born into the (employee's last name) family. We hope that the years ahead will be bright and happy ones for all of you. Your colleagues here at the firm are very happy for you and your family.

On behalf of (Firm Name), I extend our warmest wishes to you, your [wife OR husband], and baby (baby's name).

Sincerely,

FIRM NAME

Lawyer Name

Congratulations/"Pat on the Back" No. I
(Crisis Situation)

FIELD {Date}

FIELD {Name}
FIELD {Company Name}
FIELD {Address}
FIELD {City, State, Zip Code}

Dear FIELD {Salutation}:

I wanted to take this opportunity to commend you for the way you handled the emergency that occurred yesterday at the firm.

The [paramedics OR police OR firemen OR (other person)] informed us that had you not acted as quickly as you did, (state nature of the crisis situation) could have been much worse and resulted in (specify). Thank you for taking action and avoiding what could have been a much more serious situation.

On behalf of the partners, I want to tell you how proud we are of your actions and of your association with (Firm Name).

Sincerely,

FIRM NAME

[Managing Partner OR
Executive Director]

cc: (Employee Name) Personnel File
    Partners

CHAPTER

2

LETTERS FOR
LAWYERS
Essential
Communications
for Clients,
Prospects, and
Others

Congratulations/"Pat on the Back" No. 2
(For Client Compliment)

FIELD {Date}

FIELD {Name}
FIELD {Company Name}
FIELD {Address}
FIELD {City, State, Zip Code}

Dear FIELD {Salutation}:

Congratulations! Enclosed is a copy of a letter I received from (person's name) at (company name). As you can see, [Mr./Ms. (last name)] was highly complimentary of the [legal services OR other service) he/she] received from you. Your performance demonstrates the quality of service that this firm strives to render to all our clients. It is obvious that [Mr./Ms. (last name)] believes that your efforts were above and beyond (his/her) expectations.

I am happy to have this opportunity to thank you for your excellent work. It is good to have you as part of our team.

As is our policy, a copy of [Mr./Ms. (last name)'s] letter will be entered into your personnel file. Keep up the good work, (employee's first name).

Sincerely,

FIRM NAME

Lawyer Name

cc: (Employee Name) Personnel File
    Partners

Congratulations/"Pat on the Back" No. 3
(General)

FIELD {Date}

FIELD {Name}
FIELD {Company Name}
FIELD {Address}
FIELD {City, State, Zip Code}

Dear FIELD {Salutation}:

Congratulations on [your recent appointment to OR landing (name of new client) as a client]. Your commitment and dedication [to our firm OR to serving our clients OR other] is much appreciated.

We are proud and fortunate to have you at (Firm Name).

Again, it is a pleasure to congratulate you on a job well done. Keep up the good work.

Sincerely,

FIRM NAME

Lawyer Name

cc: (Employee Name) Personnel File
    Partners

CHAPTER

2

LETTERS FOR
LAWYERS
Essential
Communications
for Clients,
Prospects, and
Others

Congratulations/"Pat on the Back" No. 4
(Work Effort)

FIELD {Date}

FIELD {Name}
FIELD {Company Name}
FIELD {Address}
FIELD {City, State, Zip Code}

Dear FIELD {Salutation}:

Congratulations on a job well done! Your work on (matter) was excellent. You [showed OR demonstrated] care in (state positive aspect of their work). Additionally, you [stayed within budget OR delivered the work ahead of time OR (other positive statement)].

I am happy to have this opportunity to thank you for your excellent work. It is good to have you as part of our team.

Keep up the good work, (employee name).

Sincerely,

FIRM NAME

Lawyer Name

cc: (Employee Name) Personnel File
    Partners

Congratulations/"Pat on the Back" No. 5
(Work on Winning Proposal)

FIELD {Date}

FIELD {Name}
FIELD {Company Name}
FIELD {Address}
FIELD {City, State, Zip Code}

Dear FIELD {Salutation}:

The proposal and presentation you [made OR prepared OR helped to prepare] for (specify project and/or company submitted to) was truly outstanding. There is no doubt that we were awarded this project due [to your OR in no small measure to your] fine work.

On behalf of the partners, I want to extend our congratulations and heartfelt appreciation for a job well done. (If appropriate: Please accept the enclosed check as our way of saying thanks.)

Sincerely,

FIRM NAME

Lawyer Name

(Enclosure)

CHAPTER

2

LETTERS FOR
LAWYERS
Essential
Communications
for Clients,
Prospects, and
Others

Employee Promotion

FIELD {Date}

FIELD {Name}
FIELD {Company Name}
FIELD {Address}
FIELD {City, State, Zip Code}

Dear FIELD {Salutation}:

On behalf of the firm, it is my pleasure to inform you that you have been promoted to the challenging and demanding position of (specify position).

This promotion recognizes the fine work you have done for the firm. We are very confident that you will meet the challenges associated with your new responsibilities with the same level of energy and enthusiasm that you have demonstrated in the past.

Congratulations and good luck as you assume your new position.

Sincerely,

FIRM NAME

Lawyer Name

Employment Interview Confirmation

FIELD {Date}

FIELD {Name}
FIELD {Company Name}
FIELD {Address}
FIELD {City, State, Zip Code}

Dear FIELD {Salutation}:

This letter confirms our meeting with you on (date of appointment) at (time of appointment) at (location of appointment). I expect the interview to take approximately (length of time).

The meeting will give us the opportunity to get to know you better and to offer you some insight regarding (Firm Name), our people, and our goals.

[I OR We] look forward to seeing you on (date).

Sincerely,

FIRM NAME

Lawyer Name

CHAPTER

2

LETTERS FOR
LAWYERS
Essential
Communications
for Clients,
Prospects, and
Others

Employment Interview Request

FIELD {Date}

FIELD {Name}
FIELD {Company Name}
FIELD {Address}
FIELD {City, State, Zip Code}

Dear FIELD {Salutation}:

On behalf of (Firm Name), I would like to extend to you an invitation to interview with our firm for the position of (position).

The interview will give us an opportunity to get better acquainted and to discuss the position in greater detail. Additionally, we hope to afford you more insight into our company and our people.

Please call [me OR name of other person] at (phone number) to set up a convenient time to meet.

I look forward to meeting you.

Sincerely,

FIRM NAME

Lawyer Name

Employment Letter

FIELD {Date}

FIELD {Name}
FIELD {Company Name}
FIELD {Address}
FIELD {City, State, Zip Code}

Dear FIELD {Salutation}:

(Firm Name) is pleased to confirm your employment as (specify). You will report directly to (name of supervisor), commencing with your start of employment on (date). As with all of our employees, your first ninety days will be a probationary period.

Your salary will be $_____ per year. You will also be covered by the firm's standard group benefit plans. Fringe benefits were explained to you and you received a copy for your files. You will be entitled to (specify number) weeks of vacation per year, pro rated on a monthly basis.

If you agree that the terms set out in this letter set forth our mutual under-standing, please sign the enclosed copy and return it to (identify person) for our files.

Again, we are delighted that you have agreed to join the (Firm Name) team, and we look forward to a long and mutually beneficial association.

Sincerely,

FIRM NAME

[Lawyer Name OR
Staff Member Name]

CHAPTER

2

LETTERS FOR
LAWYERS
Essential
Communications
for Clients,
Prospects, and
Others

"Get Well" to Sick Employee

FIELD {Date}

FIELD {Name}
FIELD {Company Name}
FIELD {Address}
FIELD {City, State, Zip Code}

Dear FIELD {Salutation}:

We miss you!

This is just a short note to let you know that we here at (Firm Name) are thinking of you and wishing you a speedy recovery.

We look forward to seeing you soon. In the meantime, if there is anything we can do for you, please let us know.

Sincerely,

FIRM NAME

Lawyer Name

Jury Duty Postponement Request

FIELD {Date}

FIELD {Name}
FIELD {Company Name}
FIELD {Address}
FIELD {City, State, Zip Code}

Dear FIELD {Salutation}:

(Name of employee) of this firm has received a summons to serve as a juror, beginning (date).

The timing of (name of employee)'s jury duty creates serious problems for our firm. Since (name of employee) is currently involved in a project that requires [his OR her] specialized knowledge and expertise, it would be unlikely that we could complete this work on time if [he OR she] were absent on the date specified.

Therefore, we respectfully request that (name of employee)'s jury duty be postponed until after (date).

Thank you for your consideration in this matter.

Sincerely,

FIRM NAME

Lawyer Name

CHAPTER

LETTERS FOR
LAWYERS
Essential
Communications
for Clients,
Prospects, and
Others

Merger Memo to Employees

To: Attorneys and Staff

From: Managing Partner Name

Date:

Subj: [Pending Merger OR Merger Discussions]

I recognize that there is a high degree of anxiety over the [proposed OR planned] merger with (name firm) law firm. In order to put the rumors to rest and allay people's fears, I have called a meeting of all attorneys and staff to discuss the situation. I scheduled [a meeting OR several meetings to accommodate everyone] as follows:

(List time, date, location, and who should attend each meeting, if more than one.)

[I OR Members of the Management Committee] will discuss the status of the merger, explain what [brought it about OR led to discussions of a merger], and answer questions. Please plan to attend this very important meeting. Thank you.

New Employee Welcome

FIELD {Date}

FIELD {Name}
FIELD {Company Name}
FIELD {Address}
FIELD {City, State, Zip Code}

Dear FIELD {Salutation}:

Congratulations! On behalf of the partners and everyone at (Firm Name), it is a pleasure to welcome you to the firm. We are delighted that you have chosen to accept our offer of employment.

Our mission at (Firm Name) is to provide our clients with the best possible legal services available today. We are proud of the fine reputation we enjoy in the community (or communities where we have offices), and know that you will add much to the quality of the services we provide our clients.

We have every confidence in your ability and are happy to have you as a part of our team. Welcome!

Sincerely,

FIRM NAME

[Lawyer Name OR
Senior Staff Member Name]

CHAPTER

2

LETTERS FOR
LAWYERS
Essential
Communications
for Clients,
Prospects, and
Others

Reference No. 1– Employee Moving

FIELD {Date}

FIELD {Name}
FIELD {Company Name}
FIELD {Address}
FIELD {City, State, Zip Code}

Dear FIELD {Salutation}:

(Employee Name) has been with our firm for [several OR many OR (number of years)] and has been one of our outstanding employees in (specify department or area). For family reasons, (he/she) is moving to your area and we are truly sorry to lose (him/her).

(He/She) is a very talented individual with excellent qualities and a solid work ethic. I can truly say that any firm that hires (her/him) will have gained a great employee.

If you would like to discuss (employee name)'s qualifications further, please call me. I will be happy to share this firm's experience with (her/him) in more detail.

Sincerely,

FIRM NAME

Lawyer Name

Reference No. 2–
Employment Verification Only

FIELD {Date}

FIELD {Name}
FIELD {Company Name}
FIELD {Address}
FIELD {City, State, Zip Code}

Dear FIELD {Salutation}:

In response to your request for verification of employment for (former employee's name), our records indicate that (he/she) worked for us from (date) to (date). (He/She) held the position of (specify).

I hope this information is helpful to you. It is our firm's general policy not to offer comments in regard to a previous employee's quality of work during employment with our firm. Therefore, the above is all the information I can provide you on [Mr./Ms. (former employee's last name)].

Sincerely,

FIRM NAME

Lawyer Name

CHAPTER

2

LETTERS FOR
LAWYERS
Essential
Communications
for Clients,
Prospects, and
Others

Regret Employee Resignation

FIELD {Date}

FIELD {Name}
FIELD {Company Name}
FIELD {Address}
FIELD {City, State, Zip Code}

Dear FIELD {Salutation}:

It is with [deep regret OR regret] that I accept your resignation on behalf of the firm. We will miss you.

We recognize that change is part of everyday life and things do not stay the same. Nonetheless, we are sorry to lose you, and wish you the very best in your future endeavors.

Please keep in touch.

Sincerely,

FIRM NAME

Lawyer Name

"Thank You for the Interview"–
No Offer

FIELD {Date}

FIELD {Name}
FIELD {Company Name}
FIELD {Address}
FIELD {City, State, Zip Code}

Dear FIELD {Salutation}:

Thank you for taking the time to meet with us [yesterday OR today OR recently] regarding the (position name) position.

After discussing your qualifications and professional goals with our management team, we regret that we cannot take advantage of your talents at (Firm Name). However, with your background and experience, I am sure you will find a very satisfying position that will utilize your impressive credentials.

(Optional: We will keep your résumé in our active file in the event that another position becomes available.)

Thank you, again, for taking the time to meet with us. We wish you the best in your future endeavors.

Sincerely,

FIRM NAME

Lawyer Name

CHAPTER

2

LETTERS FOR
LAWYERS
Essential
Communications
for Clients,
Prospects, and
Others

"Thank You for the Résumé"– No Interview or Offer

FIELD {Date}

FIELD {Name}
FIELD {Company Name}
FIELD {Address}
FIELD {City, State, Zip Code}

Dear FIELD {Salutation}:

Thank you for forwarding a copy of your résumé and for expressing your interest in (Firm Name).

While you have an impressive background, we [regret to inform you that we have no openings in our firm for someone with your background OR are not hiring any new staff professionals OR anyone with your level of expertise] at this time. However, we will keep your résumé on file in the event that a position becomes available.

Best wishes to you in your future endeavors.

Sincerely,

FIRM NAME

Lawyer Name

Communication with Prospective Clients and Other Contacts

S ince first impressions are lasting impressions, your written communications with prospective clients and other contacts must be of the highest caliber. Capitalize on your opportunity to make a favorable first impression!

Although there are numerous avenues to reach prospective clients and others, this chapter provides sample letters for sending a complimentary copy of your firm's newsletter, confirming a meeting with a prospective client, or offering congratulations. There are examples of direct mailings and several follow-up letters. You will also find an announcement of the arrival of a new partner or associate and letters concerning requests for proposals (RFPs) and presentations. Also included is a letter you can use to request a rating review by Martindale-Hubbell. There are seminar invitations and seminar follow-up, letters concerning speaking engagements and sponsorships, and letters of thanks.

The letters in this chapter were designed to help you to project a professional image in your written communications with prospective clients, as well as with referral sources and others you encounter in your professional life.

CHAPTER

3

LETTERS FOR
LAWYERS
Essential
Communications
for Clients,
Prospects, and
Others

Complimentary Copy of Firm Newsletter

FIELD {Date}

FIELD {Name}
FIELD {Company Name}
FIELD {Address}
FIELD {City, State, Zip Code}

Dear FIELD {Salutation}:

Enclosed is a copy of the firm's (newsletter name). The newsletter is intended to keep our clients and other contacts informed on issues that may be of particular interest to them. I hope you find the newsletter informative.

We also send the newsletter out electronically by e-mail. If you would like to receive our newsletters, please provide us with your e-mail address [or go to our web site at www.(FirmName).com and sign up for our various newsletters online].

Our newsletter is a way for us to keep our clients and friends informed. If you do not wish to receive our newsletter on (subject), please let me know and I will remove your name from our mailing list.

Sincerely,

FIRM NAME

Lawyer Name

Enclosure

Confirmation of Meeting with Prospective Client

FIELD {Date}

FIELD {Name}
FIELD {Company Name}
FIELD {Address}
FIELD {City, State, Zip Code}

Dear FIELD {Salutation}:

I enjoyed talking with you [yesterday OR today OR on (day)]. Our firm welcomes the opportunity to discuss how we can assist [you OR (company name)] with [your OR your company's] particular legal needs.

I look forward to meeting with you on (day/date/time), at [your OR our] office. We are located at (address) (if applicable).

I have enclosed [our firm literature OR the latest issue of our client newsletter OR our statement of qualifications] for your review. I hope this will help you gain a better understanding of (Firm Name).

If you have any questions prior to our meeting, please call me. I look forward to seeing you on (date).

Sincerely,

FIRM NAME

Lawyer Name

CHAPTER

3

LETTERS FOR
LAWYERS
Essential
Communications
for Clients,
Prospects, and
Others

Congratulations–New Venture
(Business Prospect)

FIELD {Date}

FIELD {Name}
FIELD {Company Name}
FIELD {Address}
FIELD {City, State, Zip Code}

Dear FIELD {Salutation}:

On behalf of (Firm Name), I extend our congratulations to you on [the opening of your new business venture OR state name of business opportunity]. We wish you success as you undertake this new endeavor.

Starting a new [business OR venture] in today's complex business environment can be very challenging. A wise business owner chooses a team of professional advisors to help minimize risk and maximize success.

At (Firm Name), we have served businesses such as yours for more than (number of years) years. Our client base reflects our broad array of legal services, including (state services offered). We are fortunate to have experienced attorneys who are well versed in [industry OR profession] and would be happy to assist you with any legal questions.

We extend our best wishes for success in your new venture. If (Firm Name) can ever be of service to you, I hope you will call me.

Sincerely,

FIRM NAME

Lawyer Name

Congratulations–General

FIELD {Date}

FIELD {Name}
FIELD {Company Name}
FIELD {Address}
FIELD {City, State, Zip Code}

Dear FIELD {Salutation}:

Congratulations on your [recent press coverage OR appointment to (specify) OR promotion OR similar]! [It is indeed an honor OR What excellent media exposure OR What an opportunity] for you and (company name).

On behalf of everyone here at (Firm Name), we wish you continued success and prosperity in the future.

Sincerely,

FIRM NAME

Lawyer Name

CHAPTER

3

LETTERS FOR
LAWYERS
Essential
Communications
for Clients,
Prospects, and
Others

Congratulations–General
(Send with Promotional Material)

FIELD {Date}

FIELD {Name}
FIELD {Company Name}
FIELD {Address}
FIELD {City, State, Zip Code}

Dear FIELD {Salutation}:

Congratulations on your [recent press coverage OR appointment to OR promotion OR other occasion]! I am happy to hear that [you OR you and (company name)] are doing so well.

(Firm Name) takes pride in providing quality legal services to our clients. Enclosed you will find a copy of our [firm OR practice area] brochure. Should you require the assistance of an attorney, please keep us in mind.

Again, congratulations on [your OR your company's] continued [success OR triumphs OR endeavors].

Sincerely,

FIRM NAME

Lawyer Name

Congratulations–
Office Move or Expansion

FIELD {Date}

FIELD {Name}
FIELD {Company Name}
FIELD {Address}
FIELD {City, State, Zip Code}

Dear FIELD {Salutation}:

Congratulations on [your move to new offices OR the expansion of your firm]! Although it must be hectic, it is always exciting to relocate to [new OR more spacious] surroundings.

We at (Firm Name) pride ourselves on representing many successful, growing companies. I have taken the liberty of enclosing [materials about our firm OR a firm brochure] for your information. I hope you will keep us in mind if [you have OR your company has] the need for legal services in the future.

Again, congratulations and best wishes for continued success. Please contact me if our firm could be of assistance to you.

Sincerely,

FIRM NAME

Lawyer Name

Enclosure

Direct Mail No. 1–Networking

(General)

PTER

LETTERS FOR
LAWYERS
Essential
Communications
for Clients,
Prospects, and
Others

FIELD {Date}

FIELD {Name}
FIELD {Company Name}
FIELD {Address}
FIELD {City, State, Zip Code}

Dear FIELD {Salutation}:

I am writing [to introduce myself OR to you] at the suggestion of (name of person) with [(company) OR (firm) OR (specify connection)]. (Person's first name) was kind enough to mention that you might be someone [able to use my/our services OR interested in using the services of our firm OR who would appreciate learning about my firm and its services].

(Name of firm) provides [a broad spectrum of legal services OR (identify areas of services)] to a varied client base throughout [the area OR city OR other]. We have served the legal needs of various industries and professions [related to OR similar to] your [organization OR company].

Most importantly, we place the highest standards on our legal products, and we are dedicated to providing quality service in a timely and cost-effective manner. Our clients are entitled to no less.

For your information, I have enclosed a brochure which outlines the legal services provided by (Firm Name). I would welcome the opportunity to discuss our services with you, to determine how we might be able to assist you with your legal needs.

Please let me know if [you are interested in learning more about (Firm Name) OR we can be of service in any way]. Feel free to call me at (telephone number).

> Sincerely,
>
> FIRM NAME
>
> Lawyer Name

Enclosure

Direct Mail No. 2–
Mutual Friend or Client

FIELD {Date}

FIELD {Name}
FIELD {Company Name}
FIELD {Address}
FIELD {City, State, Zip Code}

Dear FIELD {Salutation}:

(Referral person's name), [a client of our firm OR our mutual friend], suggested I contact you and let you know about the legal services offered by my firm. (Discuss the relationship with client OR mutual friend.)

Enclosed is information about our firm and the services we provide in the area of (specify). I would welcome the opportunity to meet with you to discuss how (Firm Name) could assist [you OR your company] with [your OR its] legal needs.

I look forward to hearing from you, if (Firm Name) can assist you in any way.

Sincerely,

FIRM NAME

Lawyer Name

Enclosure

CHAPTER

3

LETTERS FOR
LAWYERS
Essential
Communications
for Clients,
Prospects, and
Others

Direct Mail No. 3 – Cold Call

FIELD {Date}

FIELD {Name}
FIELD {Company Name}
FIELD {Address}
FIELD {City, State, Zip Code}

Dear FIELD {Salutation}:

Enclosed is a (Firm Name) brochure. The firm offers [services in (specify practice areas) OR a broad range of legal services].

I will be in (location) on (day/date) and would enjoy meeting you to discuss the services offered by (Firm Name).

OR

If I can be service to you in meeting your legal needs, please call me at (telephone number).

OR

I will call you next week to see if you have received these materials and have any questions. I look forward to talking with you.

Sincerely,

FIRM NAME

Lawyer Name

Enclosure

Direct Mail No. 4 – Follow-up

FIELD {Date}

FIELD {Name}
FIELD {Company Name}
FIELD {Address}
FIELD {City, State, Zip Code}

Dear FIELD {Salutation}:

I wrote to you recently about the legal services available at (Firm Name). Knowing how busy people get, I thought I would follow up to see if you had any questions or if I could provide additional information.

Additionally, by way of introducing you to our firm, please sign up for any of the firm's [newsletter(s) OR advisories OR legal updates on various (specify) legal topics]. If you would be interested in receiving our newsletter(s), [please let me know OR sign on our web site at www.xxx.com].

Please let [me OR my secretary, (name),] know if you would like au: someone? to contact you about our firm's services.

Sincerely,

FIRM NAME

Lawyer Name

CHAPTER

3

LETTERS FOR
LAWYERS
Essential
Communications
for Clients,
Prospects, and
Others

Firm Name Change Letter to Non-Clients

FIELD {Date}

FIELD {Name}
FIELD {Company Name}
FIELD {Address}
FIELD {City, State, Zip Code}

Dear FIELD {Salutation}:

As our new letterhead indicates, we have recently changed the name of our firm. (State reason for the change.)

While we may have changed our name, there is no change in our commitment to providing quality legal services to our clients. Enclosed is a new firm [brochure OR résumé] which will give you some idea of the legal services we provide. If (Firm Name) can ever assist [you OR your company] with [your OR its] legal needs, please let me know. I would be pleased to explain our services in more detail.

Sincerely,

FIRM NAME

Lawyer Name

Enclosure

Follow-up with Prospective Client No. 1
(General)

FIELD {Date}

FIELD {Name}
FIELD {Company Name}
FIELD {Address}
FIELD {City, State, Zip Code}

Dear FIELD {Salutation}:

As a follow-up to our earlier discussions about a possible professional working relationship, I have enclosed some additional information about the firm.

(Firm Name) has been in business for (specify number) years and has a varied client base. Our experience is broad and includes the areas of (state practice areas). Our philosophy is simple: to provide quality legal services in an efficient and cost-effective manner to each of our clients.

[I OR We] would welcome the opportunity to provide [you OR your company OR organization] with the highest level of legal services available. I will call you next week to answer any questions you may have.

Sincerely,

FIRM NAME

Lawyer Name

Enclosure

CHAPTER

3

LETTERS FOR
LAWYERS
Essential
Communications
for Clients,
Prospects, and
Others

Follow-up with Prospective Client No. 2
(After Meeting)

FIELD {Date}

FIELD {Name}
FIELD {Company Name}
FIELD {Address}
FIELD {City, State, Zip Code}

Dear FIELD {Salutation}:

Thank you for taking time away from your busy schedule to meet with [me OR us] today.

Our firm's ability to provide quality legal service in a timely manner is our first priority. We take a personal interest in our clients and work hard to help them succeed.

As we discussed, [I will contact you regarding the (specify question) OR problem we reviewed at our meeting OR I will forward a proposal to you based on our meeting] by (day/date). If in the meantime you have any questions, please do not hesitate to call me at (telephone number).

Sincerely,

FIRM NAME

Lawyer Name

Legal Services Proposal – Follow-up

FIELD {Date}

FIELD {Name}
FIELD {Company Name}
FIELD {Address}
FIELD {City, State, Zip Code}

Dear FIELD {Salutation}:

(Firm Name) would be pleased to provide legal services to [you OR your company]. Since I have not heard from you, I assume that you have not made a decision regarding our proposal of (date) to provide legal services in the area of (practice area).

Please let me know if I can provide additional information, or respond to any questions you may have regarding our proposal.

I look forward to hearing from you at your convenience.

Sincerely,

FIRM NAME

Lawyer Name

CHAPTER

3

LETTERS FOR
LAWYERS
Essential
Communications
for Clients,
Prospects, and
Others

Legal Services Proposal – Format

I.   **Executive Summary**

II.   **Introduction**—(Indicate you are responding to [letter OR Request for Proposal], briefing who you are, due date, etc.)

III. **Understanding of [Issues OR Problem OR Situation]**—(Show that you and firm understand what the requester is asking for.)

IV.   **Approach to Be Used**—(Suggest in general terms how you or firm will approach the issues, problem, or situation.)

V.   **[Team OR Attorney] Biographies**—(Identify lawyers and paralegals, where appropriate, who will be working on the matter, and include biographies showing their experience.)

VI.   **Fee Structure**—(State how you will price the work: Mention hourly rates for both lawyers and paralegals, fixed fee, or other alternative fee arrangement.)

VII. **References**—(Without disclosing any confidential information, indicate references of other clients for whom you have done similar work.)

VIII. **General Firm Information**—(This is where the boilerplate about the firm belongs, but keep it short and relevant. Remember your Legal Bibliography course in law school, where you were told that if a Brief was supposed to be long, they would have called it a "Long.")

Note:
1. Always follow format and numbering set forth in an RFP.
2. Ask why you were not selected (and why you were) to learn how to do better in future proposals.

John B. Doe, Esq.
Doe, Dew and Dont
100 Main Street
Anytown, US 00000

Hon. Harry T. Jones
Court of Common Pleas
100 Courthouse
Anothertown, US 00001

etc.

[List a total of 10 lawyers (none from own firm) and judges. Attorneys should be "av" rated themselves. Judges are not rated.]

[**Administrative note**: Attach separate list for each attorney included in letter.]

CHAPTER

3

LETTERS FOR
LAWYERS
Essential
Communications
for Clients,
Prospects, and
Others

New Partner or Associate Announcement
(Standard Tombstone)

Whiteacre, Blackacre & Greenacre, P.C.
Attorneys-at-Law
are pleased to announce that
Thomas A. Lawyer
and
Julia S. Attorney
have been elected partners in the firm

and

Cheryl B. Smith
and
Jon Carnation
have become associates in the firm

January 1, 20XX

Pre-Proposal Information Request

FIELD {Date}

FIELD {Name}
FIELD {Company Name}
FIELD {Address}
FIELD {City, State, Zip Code}

Dear FIELD {Salutation}:

[Thank you for your request that our firm bid OR We are in receipt of your letter requesting proposals] on (name project). Our firm plans to respond [on or before (day/date) OR as soon as possible].

As we prepare our response, we would appreciate [a clarification OR further information] on the following points:
1. (Specify)
2. (Specify)
3. Etc.

Please provide this information by [telephone OR facsimile OR letter] at your earliest convenience in order that we may submit our proposal [in a timely fashion OR by the deadline].

Thank you again for this opportunity.

Sincerely,

FIRM NAME

Lawyer Name

CHAPTER

3

LETTERS FOR
LAWYERS
Essential
Communications
for Clients,
Prospects, and
Others

Proposal Presentation Letter –
Confirming Oral Presentation

FIELD {Date}

FIELD {Name}
FIELD {Company Name}
FIELD {Address}
FIELD {City, State, Zip Code}

Dear FIELD {Salutation}:

This will confirm our meeting on (Day and Date) with (names of people) at your offices to discuss our written proposal in more detail.

Our presentation team will consist of (Names of Firm Lawyers who will attend). We understand that we will be allotted one hour for our discussion. We intend to make a PowerPoint presentation, and will bring all necessary audiovisual equipment with us.

Again, thank you for this opportunity to present our credentials in more detail. We look forward to seeing you on (date).

Sincerely,

FIRM NAME

Lawyer Name

Proposal Presentation Letter – Revised Team

FIELD {Date}

FIELD {Name}
FIELD {Company Name}
FIELD {Address}
FIELD {City, State, Zip Code}

Dear FIELD {Salutation}:

This is to advise you that due to [a family emergency OR unscheduled court appearance OR other compelling reason], (Lawyer Name) will not be able to join our team at the oral presentation scheduled for (date). Rather than requesting that the meeting be rescheduled, we have added (Lawyer Name) to our team. (Lawyer's first name) is very knowledgeable in the area of (practice name) and will be a very suitable substitute to assist in explaining our written proposal in more detail.

Again, thank you for this opportunity to present our credentials and explain how (Firm Name) can serve your legal needs. We look forward to seeing you on (date).

Sincerely,

FIRM NAME

Lawyer Name

CHAPTER

3

LETTERS FOR
LAWYERS
Essential
Communications
for Clients,
Prospects, and
Others

Request for Proposal (for PR Firm)

FIELD {Date}

FIELD {Name}
FIELD {Company Name}
FIELD {Address}
FIELD {City, State, Zip Code}

Re: Request for Proposal (RFP) for Public Relations Services

Dear FIELD {Salutation}:

(Firm Name) is interested in using a public relations firm in order to raise its profile in [our market OR our various markets]. Accordingly, we are seeking a PR firm that is in the best position to assist our firm in this area.

FIRM BACKGROUND. The law firm of (Firm Name) was established in 19XX and is one of (City or State)'s prominent firms, and is currently the (XX) largest in the state. The firm has grown to over XX lawyers with offices in (location(s)).

[Here list other information that will give the PR firm a better idea of the firm and may help them prepare their proposal. Include information about the firm, well-known firm lawyers, etc.]

PHILOSOPHY. [Set forth the firm's philosophy and as much about the firm culture as possible.]

PROPOSAL REQUIREMENTS. In order to ensure that we are comparing all proposals fairly and equitably, we would appreciate your following the format below in responding to this RFP:

1. Introductory information about your firm. Please do not exceed two pages. (Additional information may be provided as an appendix.)

2. Outline of approach to providing services in accordance with the following scope of services:
   a) Placement of feature articles;
   b) Interview opportunities for key attorneys with reporters and editors;
   c) Getting selected attorneys called upon as experts in specific areas; and
   d) Draft and/or review drafts, and subsequently pitch press releases.

3. Detailed biographies, including specific media experience (whether print or broadcast) of the individuals who would be proposed for this account. Additionally, specify multi-cultural community experience.

4. The hourly rate for each person identified in 3 above.

5. Statement as to whether or not your firm would be agreeable to providing services on a project basis, hourly rate and/or retainer basis.

6. Whether your [insert name of city] area office currently represents any law firms. If so, please identify the firm(s).

7. Please provide three (3) references including contact name and telephone number.

If you choose to submit a proposal, we would appreciate receiving it no later than (date). Please submit your proposal to:

(Recipient's Name)
Firm Name
Address

Sincerely,

FIRM NAME

Managing Partner OR Marketing Director

CHAPTER

3

LETTERS FOR
LAWYERS
Essential
Communications
for Clients,
Prospects, and
Others

Request to Be Added to Request
for Proposal (RFP) List

FIELD {Date}

FIELD {Name}
FIELD {Company Name}
FIELD {Address}
FIELD {City, State, Zip Code}

Dear FIELD {Salutation}:

(Name of Firm) is a law firm with extensive experience in the areas of (specify relevant practice areas).

For many years, the firm has represented companies such as yours in (specify industry). Consequently, we understand your needs and possess the knowledge and expertise to produce the required legal services in a responsive and cost-effective manner.

Therefore, we ask that you add our firm to your RFP mailing list. Our address is:

 (Firm Name)
 (Firm Address)

We hope that you will consider our firm for [your legal needs OR your organization's legal needs]. We are happy to provide references upon request.

If you have any questions, please call me at (telephone number).

Sincerely,

FIRM NAME

Lawyer Name

Seminar Follow-up Letter No. 1
(Sending Article or Other Information)

FIELD {Date}

FIELD {Name}
FIELD {Company Name}
FIELD {Address}
FIELD {City, State, Zip Code}

Dear FIELD {Salutation}:

I am glad that you were able to attend the seminar (name, topic and date). I hope you found it informative.

As promised at the seminar, I am enclosing [an article entitled (title) about (subject) OR (other information mentioned at the seminar)]. (Expand on why the information is important.)

Again, I am happy that you were able to be with us on (date).

If you have any questions, please do not hesitate to call me.

Sincerely,

FIRM NAME

Lawyer Name

Enclosure(s)

CHAPTER

3

LETTERS FOR
LAWYERS
Essential
Communications
for Clients,
Prospects, and
Others

Seminar Follow-up Letter No. 2

(Change in Law)

FIELD {Date}

FIELD {Name}
FIELD {Company Name}
FIELD {Address}
FIELD {City, State, Zip Code}

Dear FIELD {Salutation}:

I am pleased that you were able to attend the seminar (name, topic and date). I hope you found it informative.

There has been a development since the seminar that may alter some of the information provided. [You may recall that we discussed pending legislation OR a case presently before the court.] Following the seminar, [the legislation discussed has passed the [Congress OR Legislature] and could have a significant impact on future court cases OR the (name of case) was decided by (name of court) and could have an impact on future cases in this area]. (Mention the change and implications.)

I hope you will find this update of interest, and again, I am happy that you were able to be with us on (date).

If you have any questions, please do not hesitate to call me.

Sincerely,

FIRM NAME

Lawyer Name

Seminar Follow-up Letter No. 3
(Responding to Question)

FIELD {Date}

FIELD {Name}
FIELD {Company Name}
FIELD {Address}
FIELD {City, State, Zip Code}

Dear FIELD {Salutation}:

I am glad that you were able to attend the seminar (name, topic and date). I hope you found it informative.

You may recall that a question was asked about (detail the question). I indicated that I would look into the matter and respond following the seminar. Accordingly, (set forth the answer to the question) OR (provide citation) OR (other relevant response).

Again, I am happy that you were able to be with us on (date).

If you have additional questions, please do not hesitate to call me.

Sincerely,

FIRM NAME

Lawyer Name

CHAPTER

3

LETTERS FOR
LAWYERS
Essential
Communications
for Clients,
Prospects, and
Others

Seminar Invitation
(Letter No. 1)

FIELD {Date}

FIELD {Name}
FIELD {Company Name}
FIELD {Address}
FIELD {City, State, Zip Code}

Dear FIELD {Salutation}:

I would like to extend an invitation to you and a colleague to attend a special event planned exclusively for [state type of industry OR profession OR clients]. "(Seminar Title)" will be held (date of seminar) at (location of seminar) from (beginning and ending times of seminar).

At this event you will hear specialists from the [type of industry OR profession] who will share their strategies for (state goal). (State speakers and their respective topics, if desired.)

We realize your time is limited, so [we have scheduled the event so you can get back to the office before lunch OR we are offering two sessions for your convenience OR we have scheduled the session during the evening hours OR other].

[The cost of this event is ($__) per person OR The event is complimentary to you OR our clients OR other)]. This includes handouts and [a continental breakfast of coffee, pastries, and juice OR refreshments]. To register, please complete the enclosed registration form and return it with your check payable to (specify) in the enclosed (postage paid) envelope.

I look forward to seeing you on (date of seminar).

Sincerely,

FIRM NAME

Lawyer Name

Enclosure

Seminar Invitation

(Letter No. 2)

FIELD {Date}

FIELD {Name}
FIELD {Company Name}
FIELD {Address}
FIELD {City, State, Zip Code}

Dear FIELD {Salutation}:

Enclosed is an announcement of a seminar on (topic) to be conducted at (location) on (day/date/time). The seminar is intended for (identify targeted audience). (If applicable) It has been approved for (specify) hours of [CLE OR CPE OR (specify)].

If you are interested in attending this seminar, please [send a check payable to (specify) in the amount of $_____ OR RSVP] at your earliest opportunity to reserve your place.

I look forward to seeing you on (date).

Sincerely,

FIRM NAME

Lawyer Name

Enclosure

Seminar Invitation
(Brochure/Flyer)

LETTERS FOR
LAWYERS
Essential
Communications
for Clients,
Prospects, and
Others

You Are Invited to Attend

"(Name of Seminar)"

A Seminar for [Health Care Professionals OR other]

Developed to (state goal)

(date of seminar)
(times of seminar)

At the Offices of (Firm Name)
(Firm Address) (or other location)

Presented by:
(Professional's Name)

At the seminar you will learn:
1. how to develop ( ),
2. how to use ( ), and
3. how to implement ( ).

Because of limited seating, reservations are required and are available on a first-come, first-served basis. Call (person) at (phone number) for reservations, or complete the enclosed form.

Seminar Reservation Card
(Sample)

"(Name of Seminar)"—Reservation Card

___ Yes, I will attend the seminar.

___ No, I will not be able to attend; however, please advise me of date of next seminar.

___ No, I will not be able to attend; however, please send me additional information about [the session OR the firm].

___ Enclosed is my check payable to: (Payee)

Amount Paid:

$_____ for \_\_\_\_ registrants ($_____ per person)

Name:

_____

Title:

_____

Company:

_____

Address:

_____

Telephone: _____ E-mail address: _____

Name(s) of other attendee(s):_____

For more information, please contact (contact person) at
(telephone number).

RETURN TO: (Firm Name)
              (Firm Address)

NOTE: If your firm has a web site, you may consider uploading this form so attendees can sign up and pay online.

CHAPTER

3

LETTERS FOR
LAWYERS
Essential
Communications
for Clients,
Prospects, and
Others

Speaking Engagement – Accepting

FIELD {Date}

FIELD {Name}
FIELD {Company Name}
FIELD {Address}
FIELD {City, State, Zip Code}

Dear FIELD {Salutation}:

Thank you for your kind invitation to speak before (name of group) at your (date of meeting) meeting scheduled for (time) at (location of meeting). I gladly accept your invitation.

The title of my talk is (state title). As you suggested, this will deal with (state key points of talk). Enclosed you will find my professional [biography OR credentials]. Please feel free to use this information as you prepare my introduction. If you have any questions, please contact me.

I look forward to becoming better acquainted with you and the members of your group.

Sincerely,

FIRM NAME

Lawyer Name

Enclosure

Speaking Engagement – Declining No. 1

(No Interest)

FIELD {Date}

FIELD {Name}
FIELD {Company Name}
FIELD {Address}
FIELD {City, State, Zip Code}

Dear FIELD {Salutation}:

Thank you for your kind invitation to address (name of group) at your upcoming meeting scheduled for (date) at (location of meeting). Regrettably, I am unable to accept due to a previous commitment on that date.

I wish you every success with your meeting.

Sincerely,

FIRM NAME

Lawyer Name

CHAPTER

3

LETTERS FOR
LAWYERS
Essential
Communications
for Clients,
Prospects, and
Others

Speaking Engagement – Declining No. 2
(Scheduling Conflict)

FIELD {Date}

FIELD {Name}
FIELD {Company Name}
FIELD {Address}
FIELD {City, State, Zip Code}

Dear FIELD {Salutation}:

Thank you for your kind invitation to address (name of group) at your meeting scheduled for (date) at (location of meeting).

While I would like to accept your kind invitation, I have a previous commitment on that date. However, should you [wish to have another attorney from our firm in my stead, please let me know and I will try to locate a substitute for you OR have an occasion to repeat this OR plan a similar program in the future, I would be happy to speak to your organization, if my schedule permits at that time].

I wish you every success with your meeting.

Sincerely,

FIRM NAME

Lawyer Name

Speaking Engagement – Requesting

FIELD {Date}

FIELD {Name}
FIELD {Company Name}
FIELD {Address}
FIELD {City, State, Zip Code}

Dear FIELD {Salutation}:

(Firm Name) has a long history of providing legal counsel on issues related to [state industry OR profession OR (other)]. With over (specify number) of years of experience working with individuals and businesses in the area of (specify), we believe we have provided growth opportunities for our clients and our firm.

As part of our continuing effort to inform and educate other leaders about [current legislation which may affect them personally OR professionally OR issues related to small businesses OR issues related to the (profession OR industry name) OR (other)], we would welcome an opportunity to speak to (name of organization) about the legal issues associated with (specify).

For your review, I have enclosed [our firm's OR my] [brochure OR résumé OR statement of qualifications]. Please let me know if there is interest in [me OR someone from my firm] addressing your members on (specify topic).

Sincerely,

FIRM NAME

Lawyer Name

Enclosure

CHAPTER

3

LETTERS FOR
LAWYERS
Essential
Communications
for Clients,
Prospects, and
Others

Sponsorship Letter No. 1 –
Agreeing to Sponsor

FIELD {Date}

FIELD {Name}
FIELD {Company Name}
FIELD {Address}
FIELD {City, State, Zip Code}

Dear FIELD {Salutation}:

This is in response to your letter of (date) to [me OR (name of person receiving request)] requesting that (Firm Name) sponsor (name of charitable/civic/cultural event) on (date).

Our firm is pleased to sponsor the (name of event) at the $XXXX level. Enclosed is a check in the amount of $_____ that covers our sponsorship. I understand that as part of our participation, we are entitled to a table for ten people and/or a full-page ad in the event program.

(Firm Name) is delighted to support such a worthy cause, and we look forward to a very successful event.

Sincerely,

FIRM NAME

Lawyer Name

Enclosure

Sponsorship Letter No. 2 –
Declining to Sponsor

FIELD {Date}

FIELD {Name}
FIELD {Company Name}
FIELD {Address}
FIELD {City, State, Zip Code}

Dear FIELD {Salutation}:

This is in response to your letter of (date) to [me OR (name of person receiving request)] requesting that (Firm Name) sponsor (name of charitable/ civic/cultural event) on (date).

While there are many causes worthy of our support in the community, it is impossible for us to contribute to all of them. Given our budget commitments, we unfortunately cannot lend our support to (Name of non-profit) at this time.

I want to commend all those who work so hard for (Name of non-profit) organization, and extend my very best wishes for a successful event on (date).

Sincerely,

FIRM NAME

Lawyer Name

CHAPTER

3

LETTERS FOR
LAWYERS
Essential
Communications
for Clients,
Prospects, and
Others

"Thank You"
(General)

FIELD {Date}

FIELD {Name}
FIELD {Company Name}
FIELD {Address}
FIELD {City, State, Zip Code}

Dear FIELD {Salutation}:

Please accept my sincere thanks and appreciation for (state item). I am especially grateful for the time you took to [show me the city OR take me to dinner/lunch OR meet with me OR other]. I look forward to the opportunity to return the favor.

Once again, many thanks for your kindness. I look forward to seeing you again.

Sincerely,

FIRM NAME

Lawyer Name

"Thank You"
(Event Vendors)

FIELD {Date}

FIELD {Name}
FIELD {Company Name}
FIELD {Address}
FIELD {City, State, Zip Code}

Dear FIELD {Salutation}:

(FACILITY)

Our firm held a [seminar OR reception OR (other event)] at [your hotel OR (other facility)] on (day, date). I have received a number of very favorable compliments on the event, especially regarding your courteous staff and the excellent food prepared by your [chefs OR caterer].

or

(CATERER)

Our firm held a [seminar OR reception OR (other event)] at (name facility) on (day, date). I have received a number of very favorable compliments on the event, especially on the menu you catered. Not only was the food delicious, but your staff was extremely courteous to our guests.

or

(MUSICIANS)

Our firm held a [reception OR (other event)] at (name facility) on (day, date). I have received a number of very favorable compliments on the event, including on the music your [orchestra OR band OR musicians] provided. Many people commented on how much the music added to the pleasure of the event.

I wanted to take this opportunity to thank you for your excellent contribution to the success of our (evening OR other event). Please extend our appreciation to each of those involved.

Sincerely,

FIRM NAME

Lawyer Name

Communication with the Media

M edia coverage is recognized by many lawyers as a free, third-party endorsement of their expertise, especially if they are quoted as a source or expert in news stories about their area of practice. Thus, it becomes essential for lawyers to cultivate relationships with reporters and editors in both the broadcast and print media.

The letters in this chapter will help you achieve publicity, whether the outlet be radio, television, newspapers, magazines, or trade journals. There are letters agreeing to or inviting interviews, requesting a media kit, or expressing thanks for media coverage. There is a sample firm spokesperson list, a sample media fact sheet, and a sample news release. A list of suggestions on what to do and not do in your dealings with the media should be helpful.

Achieving favorable news coverage will benefit the individual lawyer, as well as the firm's reputation. Additional benefits include creating client confidence in their choice of counsel, enhancing the firm's image in its markets, and increasing morale among the lawyers and staff because of the firm's recognition.

CHAPTER

4

LETTERS FOR
LAWYERS
Essential
Communications
for Clients,
Prospects, and
Others

Agreeing to Interview No. 1
(Radio/TV)

FIELD {Date}

FIELD {Name}
FIELD {Company Name}
FIELD {Address}
FIELD {City, State, Zip Code}

Dear FIELD {Salutation}:

Thank you for your request to interview one of our lawyers [as part of the "X" program/show OR in preparation for a broadcast] your station will be airing on (specify topic or issue).

[I OR (name of individual)] will be pleased to meet with you on (day/date) at (time) at [your station to take part in your broadcast OR (location) to provide background for the show]. [I am happy to share with you and your listeners OR viewers my insight into that area of the law OR the legal issues relating to your (specify topic of the show) OR I believe you will find him/her to be extremely knowledgeable in that area of the law and most willing to share his/her insight.]

Thank you for your interest in (Firm Name).

Sincerely,

FIRM NAME

Lawyer Name

Agreeing to Interview No. 2
(Print Media)

CHAPTER

4

Communication
with the
Media

FIELD {Date}

FIELD {Name}
FIELD {Company Name}
FIELD {Address}
FIELD {City, State, Zip Code}

Dear FIELD {Salutation}:

Thank you for your request to interview one of our lawyers for the article you are writing about (specify topic or issue).

[I OR (name of individual)] will be pleased to meet with you on (day/date) at (time) at (location). [I am happy to share with you my insight into that area of the law OR the legal issues relating to your (specify topic of article) OR I believe you will find him/her to be extremely knowledgeable in that area of the law and most willing to share his/her insight.]

Thank you for your interest in (Firm Name).

Sincerely,

FIRM NAME

Lawyer Name

CHAPTER

4

LETTERS FOR
LAWYERS
Essential
Communications
for Clients,
Prospects, and
Others

Firm Spokesperson List (Radio/TV Letter)
[OR Media Contact List]

FIELD {Date}

FIELD {Name}
FIELD {Company Name}
FIELD {Address}
FIELD {City, State, Zip Code}

Dear FIELD {Salutation}:

Enclosed is a list, organized by legal topic, of (Firm Name) lawyers who are available to assist your program hosts, reporters, and editors. Please feel free to contact any of these lawyers for the purposes of [background OR interviews] on their respective topics for any of your programs or news stories.

If you have any questions or would like the name of a lawyer specializing in any legal topic not specifically listed, please call me at (telephone number).

Sincerely,

FIRM NAME

[Managing Partner OR
Marketing/Communications Director]

Enclosure

Firm Spokesperson List
(Print Media Letter)
[OR Media Contact List]

FIELD {Date}

FIELD {Name}
FIELD {Company Name}
FIELD {Address}
FIELD {City, State, Zip Code}

Dear FIELD {Salutation}:

Enclosed is a list, organized by legal topic, of (Firm Name) lawyers who are available to assist your reporters and editors. Please feel free to contact any of these lawyers for the purposes of [background OR interviews] on their respective topics for your [newspaper OR publication].

If you have any questions or would like the name of a lawyer specializing in any legal topic not specifically listed, please call me at (telephone number).

Sincerely,

FIRM NAME

[Managing Partner OR
Marketing/Communications Director]

Enclosure

CHAPTER

4

LETTERS FOR
LAWYERS
Essential
Communications
for Clients,
Prospects, and
Others

(On Firm Letterhead)
Firm Spokesperson List
(Sample)
[OR Media Contact List]

Bankruptcy
John Jones - 000-0002

Business/Corporate
Tom Jones - 000-0007
Harriet Smith - 000-0010

Construction
Craig Painter - 000-0001

Elder Law
Buddy Meyers - 000-0004

Employment/Labor (or break down
by ADA/OSHA/FMLA/
Discrimination/etc.)
Dennis Poindecker - 000-0009
Jim Durocher - 000-0005

Environmental (or break down by
Clean Air/Superfund/Hazardous
Waste/etc.)
Nancy Brown - 000-0003
Al Schwartz - 000-0006

Estate Planning
Buddy Meyers - 000-0004
Pat Funder - 000-0011
John Blackacre - 000-0013

Government Agency Issues
Joan Singleton - 000-0021

Intellectual Property (or break
down by Patent/Copyright/
Trademark)
Oliver Wholmes - 000-0012
Jack Allen - 000-0018

Litigation
(Procedures/Process)
Judy Johnsen - 000-0014
Jeff Greenar - 000-0017

Medicaid Planning
Buddy Meyers - 000-0004

Probate
Pat Funder - 000-0014

Real Estate
Sam Slade - 000-0015

Taxation (or break down by State/
Federal/Local/Property/Estate/
etc.)
Trudy Moneyecker - 000-0016

ETC.

Inviting a Media Interview

FIELD {Date}

FIELD {Name}
FIELD {Company Name}
FIELD {Address}
FIELD {City, State, Zip Code}

Dear FIELD {Salutation}:

[With the new tax season approaching OR With the passage of the new (specify) legislation OR enactment/amendment to (specify) regulations] will come a variety of questions and concerns from your [viewers OR listeners OR readers] about their individual and business [tax OR other] liability.

Enclosed you will find a fact sheet and brochure about (Firm Name), which may be helpful in providing background on our services in this area of the law. Please feel free to utilize our resources and expertise when you need professional advice in the areas of (specify applicable practice areas). We would be happy to assist you in your preparation of [articles OR stories] on topics in [this OR these] area(s), and to make our professionals available for personal interviews with your reporters and editors, if you would so desire.

Please contact me personally at (phone number) whenever we can be of assistance to you or your [station OR publication].

Sincerely,

FIRM NAME

Lawyer Name

Enclosures

CHAPTER

4

LETTERS FOR
LAWYERS
Essential
Communications
for Clients,
Prospects, and
Others

Media Fact Sheet

(Cover Letter)

FIELD {Date}

FIELD {Name}
FIELD {Company Name}
FIELD {Address}
FIELD {City, State, Zip Code}

Dear FIELD {Salutation}:

Enclosed is a fact sheet on [our firm OR the law firm of (Firm Name)]. This background information may be [a helpful addition to the enclosed news release OR useful prior to our meeting scheduled for (day/date/time)].

If you have any questions or need additional information, please feel free to call me at (telephone number).

Sincerely,

FIRM NAME

Lawyer Name

Enclosures

Media Fact Sheet
(Sample)

Whiteacre, Blackacre & Greenacre
1234 Main Avenue, Suite #1
Anytown, US 00000   *Or*   (PUT ON FIRM LETTERHEAD)
Tel: 000-0001
FAX: 000-0002

Contact Attorneys	Practice Area	Telephone	E-mail
Tom Jones	Environmental	(101) 543-1234	tjones@firm.com
Harriet Smith	Merger/Acquisitions	(101) 543-2112	hsmith@firm.com
Buddy Meyer	Sarbanes-Oxley Act	(101) 543-2347	bmeyer@firm.com
John Blackacre	Etc.	Etc.	Etc.
Oliver Wholmes			
Judy Lawyer			
Sam Slade			
Trudy Moneyecker			
Etc.			

Client Industries Served:
Health Care
Financial Services
Manufacturing
Automobile Dealerships
Distribution
High Tech
Etc.

General Information:
Multi-practice Law Firm
Founded in 1975
7 Partners
15 Associates
20 Staff Employees

Services Provided:
(send copy of brochure)
Business/Corporate
Environmental
Estate Planning and Probate
Litigation (State and Federal Courts)

CHAPTER

4

LETTERS FOR
LAWYERS
Essential
Communications
for Clients,
Prospects, and
Others

Media Kit Request

FIELD {Date}

FIELD {Name}
FIELD {Company Name}
FIELD {Address}
FIELD {City, State, Zip Code}

Dear FIELD {Salutation}:

Our firm is giving consideration to advertising in your [publication OR newspaper OR newsletter OR journal].

Please forward a media kit, with rates and any demographic information about your readership. Additionally, if not included in the kit, please provide information about your circulation and whether such is audited.

Thank you for your attention to this request. I look forward to hearing from you.

Sincerely,

FIRM NAME

Lawyer Name

News Release
(Sample)

(On Letterhead)

NEWS RELEASE

For Immediate Release
Contact: Joan L. Stoldt
123-111-9900

William J. Byron appointed to
WHITE HOUSE CONFERENCE ON AGING

Anytown, US—(Date)—Governor George Washington appointed William J. Byron, a partner in the law firm of Whiteacre, Blackacre & Greenacre, to be a delegate to the White House Conference on Aging to begin April 15, 20xx, in Washington, D.C. Byron was the only Anytownian invited to take part in the Conference planning meeting, which was sponsored by the Upstate State Bar last month in Miami. The upcoming Conference will confront the many issues facing the aging population in the United States today.

Byron, whose practice focuses on estate planning, probate, and Medicaid planning issues, is a member of the National Academy of Elder Law Attorneys (NAELA). He is a graduate of Hardknocks University Law School and is a frequent speaker on estate planning and Medicaid topics. He will be a presenter at the Southern California Mini-Conference on Aging and Business scheduled to begin on May 9, 19xx, in beautiful downtown Burbank. He also serves on the boards of the Arthritis Foundation of Anytown and the Anytown Aging Agency, and is a member of the Association of Philanthropic Homes for the Aging and the State Health Care Association.

The law firm of Whiteacre, Blackacre & Greenacre practices in the areas of business, construction, corporate, creditors' rights, bankruptcy, elder law, employment, environment, estate planning, intellectual property, litigation, Medicaid, probate, real estate, and taxation. Visit their web site at www.wbg.com.

###

CHAPTER

4

LETTERS FOR
LAWYERS
Essential
Communications
for Clients,
Prospects, and
Others

Suggestions for Dealing with the Media

1. Send news releases to the following people (learn to be attentive to deadlines):
   a. Print—Business/Financial/Legal Editor(s) and Calendar of Events Editor (for seminars)
   b. Radio (for seminars)—Public Service Director or Community Service Director
   c. Television (for seminars)—Public Service Director and Community Relations/Service Director.

2. News releases should be written only for NEWSWORTHY items, such as:
   a. Promotions (partners, associates, and staff)
   b. Open houses or receptions
   c. Seminars
   d. Awards received by lawyers
   e. Lawyer organizational activity/offices held
   f. Research work or special studies completed by the firm
   g. Anything else truly newsworthy

3. Tips on writing an effective news release:
   a. Keep the release as short as possible (preferably under one page and no more than two pages, single-sided only).
   b. Double-space the release, 1.5"-2" margins.
   c. Enclose 3" x 5" black-and-white photograph(s) whenever possible (label the photos on the back).
   d. Address and forward the release to the appropriate person.
   e. Avoid trite, self-serving or "sales-type" comments and statements.
   f. Headline should be short and to the point.
   g. Answer who, what, when, where, why, and how in the first paragraph.
   h. Add more detail in each of the subsequent paragraphs.

4. When a media representative calls you for a quote or an interview:
   a. Return telephone calls promptly (if they don't hear from you right away, they will call another firm).
   b. Fax additional information to them as needed.
   c. Don't ask them for a "tearsheet" of the article, but do ask them to run quotes by you.
   d. Send them a statement of qualifications and/or firm literature if they don't already have these materials.
   e. Send them a follow-up note thanking them for the opportunity to be of assistance.

"Thank You" to the Media

FIELD {Date}

FIELD {Name}
FIELD {Company Name}
FIELD {Address}
FIELD {City, State, Zip Code}

Dear FIELD {Salutation}:

Thank you for arranging the interview yesterday with [me OR (name of person)]. I hope that your [viewers OR listeners OR readers][will find OR found] the [tax-related OR business OR other] information both interesting and helpful.

I am pleased that [name of publication OR station] contacted our firm regarding this subject. If the firm can provide additional assistance in the future on a legal question, please do not hesitate to contact me. The firm will continue to be as responsive as possible to your questions, and we look forward to working with you again.

Sincerely,

FIRM NAME

Lawyer Name

About the Author

Thomas E. Kane, Esq. is the principal of a legal marketing consulting firm based in Florida. Prior to establishing Kane Consulting, Inc. in 2003, he served as an in-house marketer for several firms and as a consultant to the legal industry for over 17 years. His last in-house position was as chief marketing officer for a 450-lawyer firm based in Philadelphia, where he had a staff of 13 and was responsible for the firm's marketing efforts in its 12 offices.

For nearly two decades, he has been involved in all aspects of legal marketing, from training, planning, and public relations to conducting image campaigns, market research, advertising, and client feedback programs. He oversaw the development of promotional materials, newsletters, proposals and presentations, firm marketing events, and databases for his various firms.

Prior to his legal marketing experience he was the marketing manager for a very profitable high-technology division of a Fortune 300 company, and was vice president of marketing for an engineering company.

Tom graduated from the College of the Holy Cross in Worcester, Massachusetts. Following graduation, he served a tour of active duty with the U.S. Navy, including service in the Vietnam theater. After his active duty service, he attended the University of Miami School of Law, where he received both his J.D. and LL.M. degrees. He continued his naval service as a reservist, and retired from the U.S. Naval Reserve as a captain.

Following law school, he served as an Assistant Attorney General in North Carolina, where he was the state's first environmental attorney. During his 13 years of public and private law practice, he represented clients in both federal and state courts (trial and appellate), and before federal and state agencies. He is licensed to practice in North Carolina and the District of Columbia.

Other Publications Available from the
ABA General Practice Solo & Small Firm Section

Qty	Title	Product Code	Regular Price	Section Member Price	Total
_____	Letters for Litigators	5150291	$80.00	65.00	$_____
_____	Letters for Lawyers, 2nd Edition	5150290	$80.00	65.00	$_____
_____	Package Deal: Letters for Lawyers, 2nd Edition and Letters for Litigators	5150292P	$128.00	104.00	$_____
_____	Real Estate Closing Deskbook, 2nd Edition	5150289	$99.95	85.00	$_____
_____	Attorney and Law Firm Guide to the Business of Law, 2nd Edition	5150286	$119.95	99.95	$_____
_____	Commercial Real Estate Law Practice Manual with Forms	5150287	$179.95	149.95	$_____
_____	The Lawyer's Guide to Negotiation	5150285	$79.95	59.95	_____
_____	The Effective Estate Planning Practice	5150283	$109.95	89.95	$_____
_____	Understanding Elder Law	5150288	$119.95	99.95	$_____
_____	Advising the Qui Tam Whistleblower	5150282	$94.95	79.95	$_____
_____	The Lawyer's Business Valuation Handbook	5130106	$124.95	114.95	$_____
_____	The Complete Guide to Divorce Practice, 2nd Edition	5150273	$125.95	115.95	$_____
_____	Going to Trial, 2nd Edition	5150277	$99.95	89.95	$_____
_____	Preparing Witnesses	5150272	$69.95	59.95	$_____

Orders   ***Shipping/Handling**
$5.00 to $9.99 . . . . $3.95
$10.00 to $24.99 . . . . $5.95
$25.00 to $49.99 . . . . $9.95
$50.00 to $99.99 . . . . $12.95
$100.00 to $349.99 . . . . $17.95
$350.00 to $499.99 . . . . $24.95
$500.00 to $999.99 . . . . $29.95
$1,000+ $34.95

****Tax**
DC residents add 5.75%
IL residents add 8.75%
MD residents add 5%

Subtotal	$_____
*Shipping/Handling	$_____
**Tax	$_____
TOTAL	$_____

PAYMENT
❏ Check enclosed (to the ABA)
❏ Visa ❏ MasterCard ❏ American Express

Name_____ Firm_____

Address_____ City/State/Zip_____

Account Number_____ Exp. Date_____

Signature_____

E-mail address_____ Phone Number_____

Mail: ABA Publication Orders, P.O. Box 10892, Chicago, Illinois 60610-0892
❖ Phone: (800) 285-2221 ❖ FAX: (312) 988-5568
E-Mail: orders@abanet.org ❖ Internet: www.ababooks.org